Contents

Grade 6

ISBN: 978-1-927042-09-0

AF207656

The Monarch Butterfly

The butterfly has long been a symbol of beauty. It has been around for nearly 50 million years. There are about 19 000 known species of butterflies. The Monarch butterfly is a member of the Danaidae family, which in turn is a member of Lepidoptera, the fourth largest order of insects. The Monarch is easily recognized by its reddish-brown wings, spotted with white dots and framed by a black border. It is commonly found in North America.

The metamorphosis and migration of the Monarch butterfly are two phenomena that make this insect one of the most interesting of all living creatures. In the caterpillar stage, the Monarch feeds on milkweed leaves and grows. It outgrows and sheds its skin a few times until it is about two inches in length. Then, it hangs upside down, sheds its skin for the last time, and enters the pupa stage. In the pupa stage, the caterpillar is encased in a jade green shell where it undergoes great transformation. After about two weeks, this hard capsule cracks open and a beautiful, fully-grown adult butterfly emerges.

Although Monarchs live in the temperate climates of North America, they cannot endure the cold temperature consistent with seasonal changes. When the days get shorter and the air gets cooler, the Monarch instinctively prepares to migrate to a warmer climate. What is truly remarkable is the distance that these tiny, apparently fragile creatures can travel. Although there is a great deal yet to be learned about this mysterious migratory flight, it is known that the Monarch butterfly will travel up to 3000 kilometres one way to reach its winter roosts. Since the Monarch does not fly at night, it covers up to 130 km in a day. Favourite southern locations for the Monarch include Florida, California, and central Mexico.

ISBN: 978-1-927042-09-0

Recalling Details

A. **Write "T" for true statements and "F" for false ones.**

1. There are about 19 000 species of butterflies. _____

2. Monarchs are recognized by their black wings with red dots. _____

3. The Monarch caterpillar sheds its skin as it grows. _____

4. The Monarch transforms into a hard capsule in the caterpillar stage. _____

5. The Monarch knows it is time to migrate when the snow falls. _____

6. Monarchs like to fly at night when it is cooler. _____

7. Monarchs can travel up to 130 km a day during migration. _____

8. A favourite migration destination for the Monarch is central Mexico. _____

Further Details

Check your answers in (A) over again. There are four false answers.

B. **Answer the following questions.**

1. Explain the metamorphosis (changes) that the Monarch butterfly undergoes.

    _____

    _____

    _____

2. What is the great mystery about the Monarch butterfly?

    _____

    _____

    _____

ISBN: 978-1-927042-09-0

Nouns as Objects

- When a **noun** receives the action of a verb in a sentence, it is the **object of the verb**.

  Example: He placed the book in the drawer.

  The noun "book" is the object of the verb "placed".

- When a **noun** follows a preposition in a phrase, it is the **object of the preposition**.

  Example: The girls of the sixth grade put on a play.

  The noun "grade" is the object of the preposition "of".

C. **Underline the nouns as objects. If they are objects of prepositions, circle the prepositions preceding them.**

1. Monarch butterflies do not fly at night.

2. He sat in the kitchen and ate the entire cake by himself.

3. He kicked the soccer ball through the goalposts.

4. The members of the team played hockey against another team.

5. He enjoyed the movie with the scary ending.

6. Get the ball before it goes on the road.

7. Of all of her friends, she liked Susan best.

8. The pianist played the piano for all the people.

9. John and Anne were late for school.

10. Never before had he worried so much about his school grades.

11. Please put this box into the drawer.

12. He is thinking of an interesting title for his new book.

ISBN: 978-1-927042-09-0

Compound Words

- A **compound word** is formed by combining two individual words to create a new word. The new word has a definition that is a blend of the meanings of the combined words.

  Example: every + where = everywhere   and   out + side = outside

D. Draw lines to match the words in Column A with the words in Column B to create compound words.

Column A		Column B
1.	fire •	• work
2.	mail •	• way
3.	out •	• place
4.	when •	• storm
5.	wild •	• less
6.	wind •	• grow
7.	home •	• box
8.	rain •	• ever
9.	drive •	• mill
10.	care •	• life

E. Think of five more compound words with "fire" and with "home".

fire

_____

_____

_____

_____

_____

home

_____

_____

_____

_____

_____

ISBN: 978-1-927042-09-0

Foxes – the New City Dwellers

Foxes are related to wolves and dogs and are found in most parts of the world. Typically, the fox hunts by night, but fox sightings on city streets in broad daylight are not uncommon. The red fox has been forced out of fast disappearing city ravines by inadequate food supplies brought on by the overpopulation of the species. Red foxes have been seen hunting on golf courses, in neighbourhood backyards, and casually strolling residential streets in the heart of cities and towns.

Foxes are territorial and generally do not stray beyond a radius of ten kilometres, but food shortage often drives them to expand their hunting area. The fox loves to eat rabbits, mice, and various rodents like squirrels, but when its favourite prey is scarce, it will resort to wild fruit and grass.

The fox is an able hunter with its exceptional sense of smell, sight, and hearing. It also has excellent speed, reaching up to 50 km per hour. This speed, coupled with its cunning nature, has made the fox the traditional prey of the English fox hunt. During a hunt, foxes retrace their steps to throw off the scent of the pursuing hounds and subsequently, hide in trees as the hounds and the hunters speed by.

Foxes usually mate for life and live approximately 10 to 12 years. They mate in the middle of winter and produce between two and eight cubs. Although foxes generally stay clear of human beings, it is advisable not to approach them. If you see a fox in your neighbourhood, it is likely that it has spotted you first and has already planned to avoid you.

ISBN: 978-1-927042-09-0

Skimming for Information

- When we **skim** for instant information, we read a passage quickly looking for the answers to factual questions.

A. **Read each question and skim immediately to find the answer. Write the short answer in the space provided.**

1. To which other animal groups are foxes related?   _____

2. At what time of day does a fox usually hunt?   _____

3. Which kind of fox is seen most often in the city?   _____

4. What is the radius of a fox's territory?   _____

5. What animals does a fox like to eat?   _____

6. How fast can a fox run?   _____

7. How long is a fox expected to live?   _____

8. When do foxes mate?   _____

9. When its prey is scarce, what will the fox turn to for food?

_____

10. How does a fox throw off the pursuing dogs during a fox hunt?

_____

Summarizing

B. **In your own words, explain how the fox has adapted to change.**

_____

_____

_____

_____

_____

ISBN: 978-1-927042-09-0

Active and Passive Voices

- The **voice** of a sentence shows the relationship between the verb and the subject.
- The **active voice** shows a person or thing doing something, while the **passive voice** focuses on the person or thing affected by something. The passive voice is formed with a form of the verb "be" followed by a verb in its past participle form.

  Examples: We built a snowman in front of our house yesterday. (active voice)
  A snowman was built in front of our house yesterday. (passive voice)

- Note that in a sentence in the passive voice, the person or thing that performs the action is often unknown or not mentioned because it is understood.

C. **Fill in the blanks with the correct forms of the verbs in parentheses.**

> Determine whether each sentence is in the active or passive voice first.

1. Foxes can (see) _____ on city streets in the day.

2. Pat (sting) _____ by a bee on the outing last week.

3. Their house (decorate) _____ for the party tonight.

4. Tomorrow, Dad (come) _____ to pick me up at four o'clock.

5. Our drawings (collect) _____ when the bell rang.

6. You (have) _____ to mix the ingredients well before cooking.

7. Look! Someone (leave) _____ the lights on after using the room.

8. Jack (help) _____ his little sister with her assignment now.

9. Carol (give) _____ a jigsaw puzzle for her birthday last year.

10. Yesterday's gathering (cancel) _____ because of the snowstorm.

11. The museum (close) _____ for renovation next month.

12. My parents and I (dine) _____ at a French restaurant last Sunday.

ISBN: 978-1-927042-09-0

Prefixes

- **Prefixes** are added to root words to alter their meanings. They sometimes create words that are opposite.

  Example: un + familiar = unfamiliar

  In this case, when a prefix is added, it creates an opposite meaning or an antonym.

D. **Add the correct prefixes to the following words to create new words.**

1. common (dis, un)

   _____

2. adequate (im, in)

   _____

3. respect (un, dis)

   _____

4. dependable (in, un)

   _____

5. dependent (un, in)

   _____

6. appear (dis, un)

   _____

7. mature (in, im)

   _____

8. pleased (dis, un)

   _____

9. certain (in, un)

   _____

10. mortal (im, in)

    _____

11. reliable (un, in)

    _____

12. tasteful (dis, un)

    _____

13. appropriate (un, in)

    _____

14. responsible (in, ir)

    _____

15. regard (ir, dis)

    _____

16. belief (un, dis)

    _____

ISBN: 978-1-927042-09-0

When Wayne Gretzky was just six years old, his father, Walter Gretzky, managed to sign him to play with the ten-year-olds in the Atom League in Brantford, Ontario, giving him his first <u>opportunity</u> to play on a team. Mr. Gretzky was an <u>avid</u> hockey fan and excellent teacher. He made a rink in his backyard where he drilled Gretzky on the basic skills and <u>instilled</u> in him the desire to practise hard and always give his all in every game.

Actually, Gretzky was too young to play organized hockey. Being so small, he had difficulty controlling his <u>oversized</u> hockey sweater which was constantly getting in the way of his stick on his shooting side. To <u>compensate</u>, Gretzky tucked in his jersey on the one side and consequently established his trademark style. Years later, thousands of young hockey players would be wearing their jerseys the same way, <u>imitating</u> the Great One.

"The Great One" —
Wayne Gretzky (1)

In his first season of organized hockey, Gretzky managed to score only one goal. However, he scored 27 in his second season, 104 in his third season, and an <u>astounding</u> 196 goals in the following season. By the time Gretzky was ten, the proper age for his league, he had established himself as a <u>prodigy</u> by scoring an incredible 378 goals in a single season. As a young hockey player, Gretzky's idol was Gordie Howe, the great Detroit Red Wings player, who held numerous scoring titles. Little did Gretzky know at the time that he would go on to <u>shatter</u> all those records and set new ones that seem <u>insurmountable</u> today.

Gretzky made his professional <u>debut</u> in 1978 at the age of 17 with the Indianapolis Racers of the World Hockey League (WHA). The Racers fell into financial trouble and had to sell Gretzky to the Edmonton Oilers. In his first season with the Oilers, Gretzky scored 43 goals and added 61 assists for a 72-game total of 104 points. When the WHA began to fall apart, the Edmonton Oilers were <u>incorporated</u> into the National Hockey League (NHL) for the 1979-80 season and, in this, his first official year in the NHL, Gretzky amassed 51 goals and 86 assists for a total of 137 points. He was voted the League's most valuable player – an honour he was to go on to achieve eight <u>consecutive</u> times.

During his years with the Oilers, Gretzky broke Phil Esposito's scoring record with 92 goals, <u>surpassing</u> the 200-point per season <u>milestone</u>. Later he established an all-time scoring record with 215 total points in a single season.

ISBN: 978-1-927042-09-0

Checking Facts

A.   Skim the passage and write short answers to the following questions.

1.   At what age did Gretzky first play organized hockey?   _____

2.   Who first taught Gretzky the game of hockey?   _____

3.   How old were Gretzky's teammates on his first organized team?   _____

4.   How many goals did Gretzky score in his first year of organized hockey?   _____

5.   Who was Gretzky's hockey idol when he was growing up?   _____

6.   How old was Gretzky when he signed his first professional contract?   _____

7.   How many points in a single season did Gretzky score to establish the all-time record?   _____

Drawing Conclusions

B.   Answer the following questions.

1.   What skills did Gretzky possess that made him such a great player?

   _____

   _____

2.   How did Walter Gretzky contribute to his son's success?

   _____

   _____

ISBN: 978-1-927042-09-0

Perfect Tenses

- The **present perfect tense** shows an action from the past that is linked to the present. It is also used for recent actions with no indication of a definite time. It is formed with "has/have" followed by the past participle of a verb.

  Examples: Grandpa <u>has planted</u> a tree in the yard.
  (Grandpa planted a tree in the past and the tree can be seen in the yard now.)

  I have seen a real polar bear before.
  (No definite time is given.)

- The **past perfect tense** shows something happened before another event in the past. It is formed with "had" followed by the past participle of a verb.

  Example: They <u>had finished</u> all decorations before the guests arrived.

- Note that the perfect tense is usually used with these words:
  already, yet, never, before, recently, lately, since, for

C.   Fill in the blanks with the verbs in the correct perfect tenses.

1. Wayne Gretzky (establish) _____ himself as a prodigy by the age of ten.

2. Ruth (not eat) _____ any meat since last week.

3. Dad (already put) _____ the garbage out.

4. After they (finish) _____ painting the fence, they played a game of soccer.

5. I really want to go to the party but I (not ask) _____ for my mom's permission yet.

6. The show (already start) _____ when we arrived at the theatre.

7. Jenna (not visit) _____ that place again ever since her favourite restaurant closed down.

8. Christine (never be) _____ to a water park before.

9. Many students (join) _____ that charity organization lately.

ISBN: 978-1-927042-09-0

New Words in Context

- When we read unfamiliar words, it is useful to use the sentence in which these words appear to help us understand their meanings. The information given in the sentence and the purpose of the sentence is its **context**.

D. Match the underlined words in the passage with their meanings.

> Read the sentence in which each underlined word appears. After you complete filling in the list, use your dictionary to check the meaning of each underlined word.

Meaning	Underlined Word
1. beginning, first time	
2. break into pieces	
3. make up for	
4. inspired, promoted	
5. very big, too large	
6. genius	
7. chance	
8. difficult to overcome	
9. keen	
10. all in a row	
11. joined, made part of	
12. overcoming, going beyond	
13. copying	
14. shocking	
15. accomplishment	

ISBN: 978-1-927042-09-0

After the 1989 Stanley Cup victory, Gretzky was traded by the Edmonton Oilers to the Los Angeles Kings, a team with a losing record and very few spectators in attendance at home games. Los Angeles was a great baseball city and the game of hockey was foreign to the people there. It was not long, however, until the citizens of Los Angeles came out to witness the greatest player to ever play the game. Gretzky did not disappoint them. In 1989, he broke Gordie Howe's lifetime scoring record of 1850 total points and went on to lead the Kings to the Stanley Cup finals. The once sparsely occupied arena in Los Angeles was then sold out for every home game as the Kings' fans embraced Gretzky.

Gretzky states in his autobiography: "The greatest game of my life might not have been a hockey game. It might have been a Celtics–Lakers game." Gretzky was in attendance at that basketball game when a beautiful young lady came over to say hello. That was the moment when Gretzky met his future wife Janet Jones, a dancer, model, and movie actress.

Gretzky has always exhibited respect for fellow NHL players and expressed admiration for past hockey greats. He openly praised the accomplishments of Gordie Howe and Jean Belliveau. He had the greatest respect for Mario Lemieux, the player thought most likely to break his scoring titles, and, of course, for his other best friend, Mark Messier. In his autobiography, Gretzky closes by listing the five players he would choose as his personal All-Star Team. In goal, he put Grant Furr and on the defence, he put Larry Robinson and Paul Coffey. His choice for forwards were Gordie Howe and Mark Messier, and at centre, he placed Mario Lemieux.

"The Great One" — Wayne Gretzky (2)

Gretzky was not very big in stature, nor was he particularly fast on skates. He did, however, have the uncanny ability to control the offence of the game. Pinpoint passing, the knack for finding his teammates, and the creativity to mastermind scoring opportunities virtually every shift on the ice account for his total domination of the game of hockey. When Gretzky retired in 1999, fans were saddened at the prospect that such a great player and ambassador of the game would never play again.

ISBN: 978-1-927042-09-0

 **The Main Idea**

A. State the main idea of each paragraph in one sentence.

Paragraph One

_____

_____

Paragraph Two

_____

_____

Paragraph Three

_____

_____

Paragraph Four

_____

_____

Making Assumptions

B. Write "agree" or "disagree" for each statement.

1. Fans will support a winning team.   _____

2. There are many great players both past and present
    in the NHL.   _____

3. Skill is more important than size.   _____

4. Gretzky is a humble individual.   _____

5. Any player, regardless of how great, can be traded.   _____

6. Gretzky will always be remembered.   _____

ISBN: 978-1-927042-09-0

Mood

- Sentences can be in one of these three **moods**:

  A statement or question is in the **indicative mood**.

  Examples: The strawberries are big and juicy.

  Did they go to the cottage last summer?

- A command or request is in the **imperative mood**.

  Examples: Don't touch the hot kettle.

  Please write your name here.

- A hypothetical case or a wish is in the **subjunctive mood**.

  Examples: If Denise had not been sick, she would have gone to the movies with us. (But she was sick and did not go to the movies with us.)

  I wish I could fly a plane.

C. **Determine whether each sentence is in the indicative (IN), imperative (IM), or subjunctive (SUB) mood.**

1. Wayne Gretzky broke Gordie Howe's lifetime scoring record in 1989.   _____

2. Leonard wished he could be a record holder.   _____

3. The new restaurant will be opened next Saturday.   _____

4. Remind Stephanie to leave the key in my drawer, please.   _____

5. Never go into that room without the teacher's permission.   _____

6. How could you find this limited edition?   _____

7. How I wish I could go to Spain with my sister.   _____

8. If she were here, she would definitely give us a hand.   _____

9. Please don't forget to bring along a pencil and a notebook.   _____

10. Is the man over there Joe's father?   _____

ISBN: 978-1-927042-09-0

New Words

D. Complete the crossword puzzle with the words from the passage on the word list below.

Word List

embraced   knack
autobiography   foreign
domination   witness
exhibited   ambassador
disappoint   stature
sparsely   uncanny

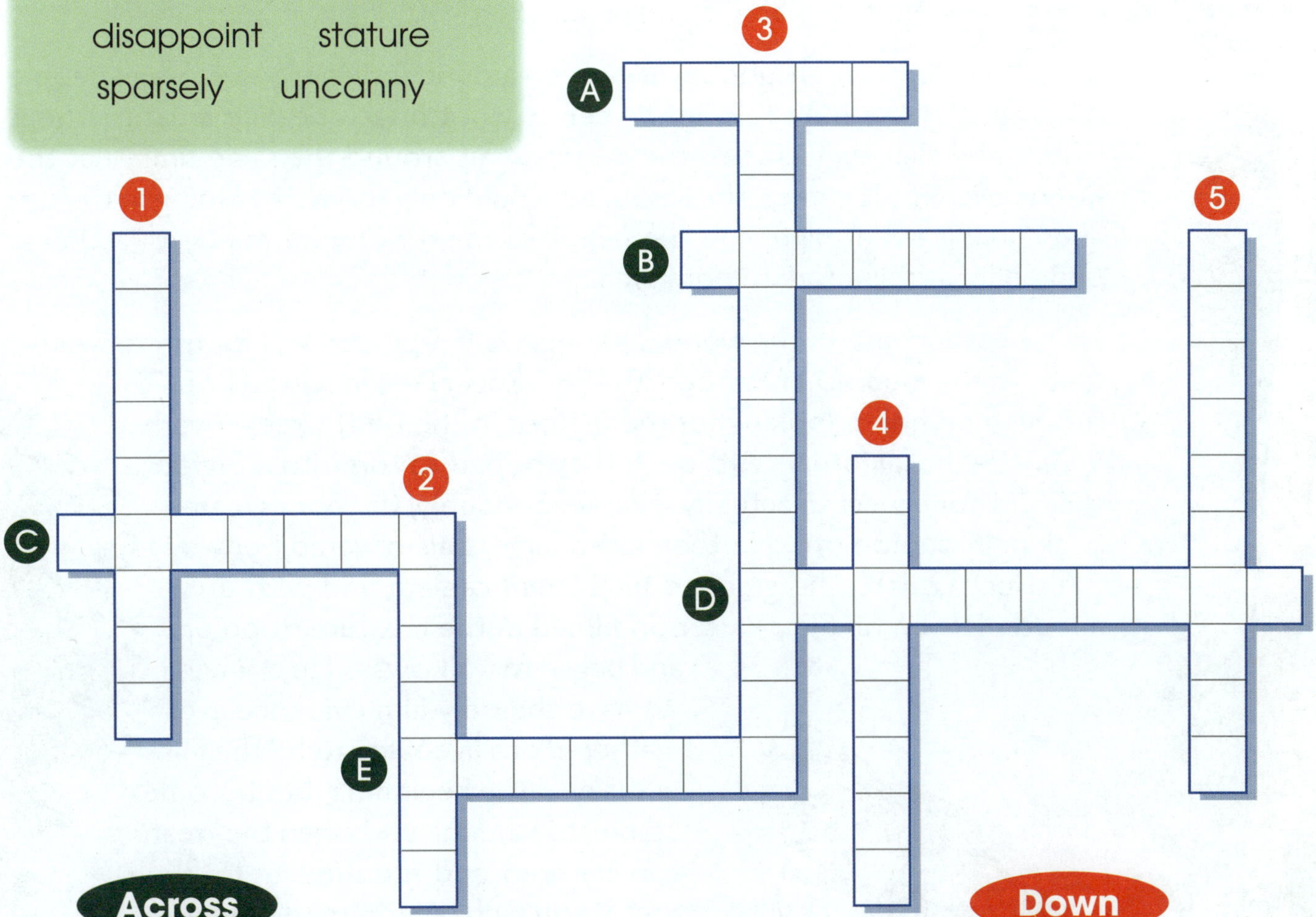

Try to figure out the meanings by reading the sentences in which these words appear. Not all of the words appear in the puzzle.

Across

A. ability to do
B. from another land
C. see it happen
D. representative
E. odd, unusual

Down

1. shown
2. physical size
3. story about self
4. held tightly
5. let someone down

ISBN: 978-1-927042-09-0

The Sasquatch –
Canada's Legendary Monster

Have you heard of a large hairy monster that lives in the woods and walks upright like a human? In some parts of Canada, it is called "Bigfoot" because of the large bare footprints it leaves in the mud. In British Columbia, it is "Sasquatch", as the Salish natives call it, which means "hairy man" or "wild man".

The Sasquatch has been described as having long arms and legs, with big hands and feet. It is over two metres tall. Some people claim to have photos of the monster, but they were usually shot from a distance and are often hard to make out.

These stories and sightings have been around for many years. Some people propose that the monsters are descendents of huge ape-like creatures from China, and that they crossed the Bering Strait around the same time that the first native people came. The Sasquatch could only survive by hiding in the day and coming out at night. As the land became developed, the Sasquatch was pushed into even more remote areas.

In other parts of the world, sightings were reported and footprints were found in the mud. On October 20, 1967, Roger Patterson and Bob Gimlin travelled on horses looking for the Bigfoot in the Bluff Creek Riverbed in Northern California. Although they hoped to run into a Bigfoot, they did not expect to actually see one. Suddenly, the horses reared, bucking Patterson off. He then saw a large, hair-covered body by the river. Quickly, he grabbed his 16 mm camera and with only minutes left on his film, Patterson filmed as the creature stood up and began to walk away. He claimed to have the only film evidence ever gathered of a live Sasquatch. The film is shaky in the beginning, but becomes stabler toward the end when the creature can be seen and identified. In 2005, the Sasquatch again made news because a piece of hair from the creature was found, but unfortunately, scientists found out that the hair was from a bison.

ISBN: 978-1-927042-09-0

 **Recalling Details**

A. Write "T" for true statements and "F" for false ones.

1. The large hairy monster is known as "Bigfoot" in British Columbia. _____

2. The Bigfoot is a hairy man. _____

3. The photos of the Sasquatch are usually not clear. _____

4. The Sasquatch is an ape from China. _____

5. The first native people brought in the Sasquatch when they came. _____

6. The Sasquatch was forced to inhabit more remote areas because of land development. _____

7. Roger Patterson went to look for the Bigfoot in Northern California alone. _____

8. Patterson filmed the Bigfoot with his 16 mm camera. _____

9. A piece of hair claimed to be from the Sasquatch was actually from a bison. _____

Further Details

B. Answer the following questions.

1. Why is the large hairy monster called "Bigfoot"?

   _____

   _____

2. Which sentence in the passage implies that the Sasquatch tries to avoid human contact?

   _____

   _____

3. Do you think the film Patterson shot should be accepted as evidence that the Bigfoot exists?

   _____

   _____

ISBN: 978-1-927042-09-0

Direct and Indirect Speech

- **Direct speech** repeats the exact words spoken by someone, and the words are put in between quotation marks.

  Example: Mom told Kelly, "Put the toys away."

- **Indirect speech** reports what someone said, and no quotation marks are needed.

  Example: Mom told Kelly to put the toys away.

- Changing direct speech to indirect speech involves tense changes. The tense in indirect speech is one tense back in time from that in direct speech.

  Example: Ryan said, "The light <u>went out</u> suddenly."
  Ryan said that the light <u>had gone out</u> suddenly.

- Note that when changing direct speech to indirect speech, there is no need to change the tense if the statement is about something that is still true or if the reporting verb is in the present tense.

  Examples: Mr. Nixon told the students, "The sun <u>is</u> a star."
  Mr. Nixon told the students that the sun <u>is</u> a star.

  Little Elf <u>says</u>, "The dragon <u>is</u> outside the castle."
  Little Elf <u>says</u> that the dragon <u>is</u> outside the castle.

C.   Write the sentences in indirect speech.

1. Mrs. Green said, "Roger Patterson saw a Sasquatch in 1967."

   _____

2. Nina told her dad, "There is a stranger outside."

   _____

3. Mom always says, "Money is not everything."

   _____

4. Kyle explained, "There are no polar bears in the South Pole."

   _____

5. "I have won the competition!" Sarah told her friends.

   _____

6. My sister told me, "Vienna is the capital of Austria."

   _____

ISBN: 978-1-927042-09-0

Suffixes

- **Suffixes** are added to root words to alter their meanings. They change the part of speech of root words, that is, how the root words are used in sentences.

  Examples: 1. retire ➔ retirement

  The root word "retire" is a verb but the new word "retirement" formed by adding the suffix "ment" is a noun.

  2. live ➔ lively

  The root word "live" is a verb but the new word "lively" formed by adding the suffix "ly" is an adjective.

D. Add the correct suffixes to the following words to create new words.

1. wicked (ment, ly)

   _____

2. simple (ent, ly)

   _____

3. pure (ance, ly)

   _____

4. confine (ly, ment)

   _____

5. glory (ment, ous)

   _____

6. treachery (ly, ous)

   _____

7. definite (ment, ly)

   _____

8. discover (ment, y)

   _____

9. invent (ion, ment)

   _____

10. heavy (ly, ous)

    _____

11. happy (ment, ness)

    _____

12. perform (ent, ance)

    _____

13. create (ive, ous)

    _____

14. major (ity, ion)

    _____

15. real (ity, ous)

    _____

16. anchor (ment, age)

    _____

> *Use your dictionary to check the spellings of the new words formed above.*

ISBN: 978-1-927042-09-0

Left Brain, Right Brain

Did you know that your brain is divided into two halves: left and right? Scientists refer to these divisions as hemispheres. Each of these hemispheres (halves) controls different functions. In the majority of people, the left side of the brain controls fine-motor activities on the right side of the body, which would account for the fact that most people are right-handed. The left side is also credited with controlling speech, the details of touch, and close vision in most people. The right side of the brain performs its own set of unique functions. You are using the right side of your brain when you can tell if someone is happy or angry by his or her face or voice.

The specialized functions of the left and right sides of the brain are called lateralization. It is the functions of these sides of the brain that determine whether or not you favour the use of your right hand, foot, eye, or ear. Researchers are very interested in studying how we perform simple tasks and why the two hemispheres of the brain work differently. They hope to understand further how the brain processes information and relays information to the body which enables us to perform tasks.

Try a simple experiment to determine how your own brain processes information. Choose a stationary object on a wall on the other side of the room. Hold up your thumb at arm's length and, with both eyes open, locate the tip of your thumb under the object. Close your left eye. Did your thumb remain in place? Now, close your right eye. Did your thumb jump to the right? Over half the population would see their thumb jump to the right. This means that your right eye is more tuned into your visual perception than your left eye. Less than 10% of the population will experience the opposite result. The remainder of the population will experience no movement at all.

Only about 12% of the world's population (or one in every eight people) is left-handed. Survey your friends, family, and classmates to determine if the statistics hold true.

ISBN: 978-1-927042-09-0

Organizing Information

A. **Make a list in the chart below of the skills and activities common to each side of the brain.**

Left Brain	Right Brain

Recalling Details

B. **Fill in the blanks with the correct words from the list below.**

> left   right   10%   hemispheres
> touch   12%   lateralization

Our brain is divided into two parts called 1._____ . The specialized functions of the left and right sides of the brain are called 2._____ . Only about 3._____ of the world's population is left-handed. In an experiment to determine how the brain processes information, less than 4._____ of the people tested would see the thumb jump to the left. Details of 5._____ are attributed to the left side of the brain. When you tell how a person feels by the expression on his or her face, you are using the 6._____ side of your brain.

ISBN: 978-1-927042-09-0

Gerund Phrases

- A **gerund phrase** is a verbal phrase that contains a gerund ("ing" form of a verb). It functions as a noun and can be the subject, object, or complement of a sentence.

  Examples: <u>Listening to the sounds of nature</u> is a good way to relax. (subject)

  Herman likes <u>playing soccer with his friends</u> after school. (object)

  Happiness is <u>having family and friends that always support you</u>. (complement)

C.   Underline the gerund phrase in each sentence and determine whether it functions as the subject (S), object (O), or complement (C) in the sentence.

1. Writing with the left hand is not an easy task for most right-handed people. _____

2. Missing the game was the player's biggest regret. _____

3. The best part of the trip was taking the cable car to the peak. _____

4. Swimming in the ocean is a very refreshing activity. _____

5. Quincy avoided eating too much fried food in order to stay fit. _____

6. My dad enjoys raking fallen leaves in the yard. _____

7. What Jacqueline wants to do most this summer is composing a memory book. _____

8. You should try solving the problem on your own first. _____

9. My favourite pastime is reading science fiction. _____

10. For Ethan, the most meaningful thing in life is doing volunteer work. _____

11. Christina's new year's resolution was working out at least four times a week. _____

12. Getting into an abandoned house in the middle of the night is not wise at all. _____

ISBN: 978-1-927042-09-0

Word Challenge

D. **Unscramble each word to form a word from the passage with the help of the clue in parentheses.**

1.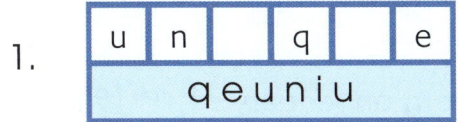

   u n _ q _ e

   q e u n i u

   (different, special)

2.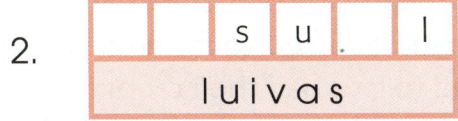

   _ _ s u _ l

   l u i v a s

   (to do with sight)

3.

   _ _ t _ r _ n e

   t e e d n r e i m

   (to decide)

4.

   e x _ e _ i _ e _ t

   t e n m i r e p e x

   (run a test)

5.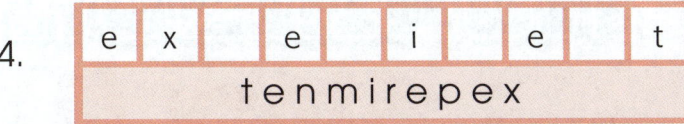

   p _ _ u _ _ t _ o _

   p i n o t a l u o p

   (all the people)

6.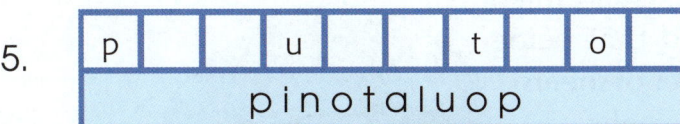

   s _ a t _ o n _ r

   y o n a r i t s a t

   (remain in one spot)

7.

   _ e r _ e _ t i _ n

   n e r p e c i o t p

   (view of something)

8.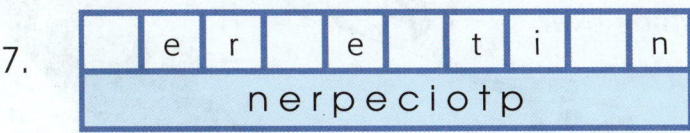

   h _ m _ s _ h e _ e s

   s i m p e h s e r e h

   (two halves)

9.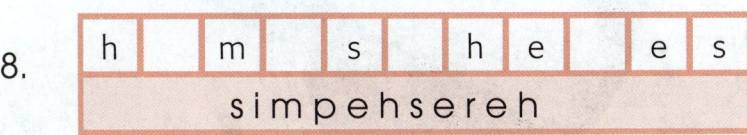

   _ _ t _ r _ l _ z _ _ i _ n

   a l z i n t t a r a e l o i

   (left or right side)

ISBN: 978-1-927042-09-0

When Jackie Robinson trotted onto Ebbets Field, home of the Brooklyn Dodgers baseball team, on April 15, 1947, professional baseball would never be the same again. On that day, Jackie Robinson became the first black American to play major league baseball, and the first brave step in breaking the colour barrier against black players was boldly taken.

Jackie Robinson was born on January 31, 1919 in an old farmhouse on the outskirts of Cairo, Georgia. His father was a sharecropper. Sharecroppers never owned the land they worked. They were allowed to farm the land owned by white landlords but had to give half their crops to the owners as rent. When Robinson was only a year and a half old, his father abandoned the family, leaving Robinson's mother alone to care for the five children.

The Jackie Robinson Story (1)

Life for a black person showed no promise in the South, so Mrs. Robinson took her family to Pasadena, California in hopes of a better life. Robinson soon learned that being black in America was not easy. He was the subject of sneers and taunts from neighbours. Mrs. Robinson taught her children to be polite and stay out of trouble but also to be proud and stand up for themselves. Robinson never forgot these important lessons that would be invaluable to him later in life. Robinson, realizing that his mother had little money, helped out by doing odd jobs in the neighbourhood and turning over his earnings to his mother.

Robinson's first baseball was a rag ball – a ball of wool wrapped in a rag. He played with it all day long and tried hitting it with a stick and found that he was quite good at doing it. When Robinson entered high school, he was immediately recognized for his athletic ability. In addition to being a track and field star, he played varsity football, basketball, and of course baseball.

ISBN: 978-1-927042-09-0

Fact or Opinion

- A **fact** is a statement that can be proven by the text of a story. An **opinion** is a person's thoughts or feelings about a subject based on what he or she has read. While opinions may be logical, they are not factual.

A. Write "F" for fact or "O" for opinion for each statement.

1. Jackie Robinson was a great baseball player. _____

2. The Robinson family was very poor. _____

3. Robinson's father was a sharecropper. _____

4. Robinson's father left them because he was tired of working. _____

5. Mrs. Robinson moved to California to start a better life. _____

6. The Robinson children were not afraid to stand up for their rights. _____

7. Robinson did not have money for baseball equipment. _____

8. Robinson first practised baseball with a rag ball. _____

9. Robinson knew as a child that he could be a ball player. _____

10. The Robinson family had too many children to look after. _____

11. The day Robinson played professional baseball was the day the game changed forever. _____

12. Robinson was glad to give his mother the money he earned. _____

B. Answer the following question with your opinion based on the facts in the passage.

What difficulties in life did Jackie Robinson have to overcome as a youth?

_____

_____

_____

_____

_____

ISBN: 978-1-927042-09-0

Participial Phrases

- A **participial phrase** is a verbal phrase that contains the present or past participle form of a verb. It functions as an adjective in a sentence.

  Examples: The girl <u>sitting on the bench</u> was waiting for her mom.
  (contains the present participle of "sit" and describes the noun "girl")

  The book <u>torn by the naughty cat</u> belonged to Penelope.
  (contains the past participle of "tear" and describes the noun "book")

- Be careful not to confuse a participial phrase with a present participle of a verb with a gerund phrase.

  Examples: <u>Jogging in the park</u>, Maggie met her neighbour. (participial phrase)
  <u>Jogging in the park</u> is good exercise. (gerund phrase)

C. Check the sentences that contain participial phrases.

1. Realizing that his mother had little money, Robinson turned over his earnings to her. _____

2. Breaking the colour barrier was Jackie Robinson's greatest achievement. _____

3. Not knowing what to do, the man just waited helplessly for rescue to come. _____

4. The organizer greeted the people attending the event. _____

5. George found a rare shell hidden in the sand. _____

D. Write sentences with the given participial phrases.

1. looking at the raccoon

   _____

2. chosen into the choir

   _____

3. left in the garage

   _____

ISBN: 978-1-927042-09-0

Antonyms

- **Antonyms** *are words that are opposite in meaning.*
  Examples: *love – hate; big – small; tall – short*

E.   Circle the antonym for each of the lead words.

1.	**vanish**	disappear	appear	show	illuminate
2.	**famous**	notorious	unknown	quiet	noisy
3.	**superb**	fair	natural	wonderful	poor
4.	**creative**	mindful	wise	dull	finicky
5.	**friendly**	happy	depressed	unsociable	naughty
6.	**rigid**	fixed	firm	flexible	tough

Prefix: "Anti"

- The **prefix "anti"** *means "against", which, when added to a word, creates an antonym.*

Use your dictionary to find the words beginning with "anti" that match the definitions.

F.   Complete the words with the prefix "anti".

1.   creates immunity to fight disease   a n t i b ☐ ☐ y

2.   not friendly   a n t i s o ☐ ☐ a ☐

3.   cleans a wound   a n t i s e ☐ t ☐ ☐

4.   prevents car engine from freezing   a n t i f ☐ ☐ ☐ z ☐

5.   to defend against aircraft attacks   a n t i a ☐ ☐ c ☐ ☐ f ☐

ISBN: 978-1-927042-09-0

In California, Robinson attended Pasadena Junior College where he set records in track and field, quarterbacked the football team, and led the basketball team in scoring. He led the Pasadena varsity baseball team to the championship and was voted MVP (Most Valuable Player). After graduation, Robinson was offered numerous scholarships to major universities. He chose UCLA where he became an athletic hero. When he joined the Kansas City Monarchs of the Negro League, he was finally being paid to do what he did best.

The Jackie Robinson Story (2)

Professional baseball was a segregated sport. Black players were prohibited from playing. On August 28, 1945, that was about to change. Branch Rickey, a forward-thinking Dodger manager, signed Jackie Robinson to a contract and sent him to play for the Montreal Royals, a Dodger farm team. On April 10, 1947, history was made. Robinson became the first black American to sign a major league baseball contract.

When Robinson stepped onto New York's Ebbets Field that opening day, he faced the jeers of the crowd. The Dodgers won the game 5-3 and Robinson set up the winning run. Over the next few seasons, he was to endure racial insults, prejudicial treatment in public places, and death threats. One teammate even requested to be traded rather than play with Robinson. The St. Louis Cardinals threatened to cancel the scheduled league game with the Dodgers if Robinson played. Robinson answered the public scorn by winning the Rookie of the Year in 1947 and going on to help the Dodgers win six pennants in ten years. He stole home base, a particularly difficult task, an unprecedented 19 times.

Robinson retired in 1956 with a lifetime batting average of 0.311. It was not until 1959, however, that all major league teams fielded at least one black player. In 1962, he was inducted into the National League Hall of Fame – the first black player to receive that honour. He is remembered as a courageous man who single-handedly broke the colour barrier in professional baseball. Robinson died in 1972. His epitaph reads: "A life is not important except in the impact it has on other lives."

ISBN: 978-1-927042-09-0

Finding Important Information

A. **Write the exact sentence from the passage that best supports each of the following statements.**

1. Jackie Robinson could play numerous sports well.

   _____

   _____

2. Robinson began to earn money as a professional baseball player.

   _____

   _____

3. One manager in professional baseball had different views from the rest.

   _____

   _____

4. Robinson endured racism against him and, by the end of the season, proved that he could play the game as well as anyone.

   _____

   _____

Reading into the Story

B. **Answer the following questions.**

1. List three qualities of character that Robinson must have possessed that helped him overcome such adversity.

   a. _____ b. _____ c. _____

2. Give examples from the passage of actions or situations that prove the above answers.

   a. _____

   b. _____

   c. _____

ISBN: 978-1-927042-09-0

Infinitive Phrases

- An **infinitive phrase** is a verbal phrase that contains an infinitive ("to" form of a verb). It functions as a noun, an adjective, or an adverb in a sentence.

  Examples: <u>To complete the task in a day</u> is impossible. (noun)

  We need another container <u>to hold the juice</u>. (adjective)

  My mother sat down <u>to lecture me</u>. (adverb)

- Note that an infinitive phrase is made up of "to" followed by a verb and other modifiers. If a noun, a pronoun, or a noun phrase follows "to", it is a prepositional phrase and not an infinitive phrase.

  Example: I go <u>to the cottage in Muskoka with my family</u> every summer. (prepositional phrase)

C. Underline the infinitive phrase in each sentence and determine whether it functions as a noun (N), an adjective (Adj), or an adverb (Adv).

1. Jackie Robinson was the first black American to sign a major league baseball contract. _____

2. Mom opened the window to let in fresh air. _____

3. They went to every park to search for their dog. _____

4. The ballerina practised every day to improve her skill. _____

5. Andy and Martin needed more time to gather information for their project. _____

6. The objective of this event is to raise funds for the organization. _____

7. To give up is not a solution to the problem. _____

8. Getting enough sleep is one of the many ways to stay fit. _____

9. The children were thrilled that they had a chance to meet the king and queen in person. _____

10. To keep experimenting is the only choice they have. _____

11. You have to read the instruction first to complete the activity. _____

12. The first step to making the dish is to get all the ingredients ready. _____

ISBN: 978-1-927042-09-0

Homophones

- **Homophones** are words that sound the same but have different meanings. Often these words are confused when we create sentences.

D. Circle the correct word in each pair of homophones to complete the sentence.

1. Jackie Robinson was a grate, great player in his time.

2. A watt, what is an electronic measurement.

3. This was the first book that he had red, read this year.

4. The boat was on sale, sail for a good price.

5. The driver did not break, brake in time.

6. The superstar accomplished another great feet, feat .

7. It never rains but it pores, pours .

8. She could not bear, bare to see the animal suffer.

E. Complete the crossword puzzle with the homophones of the given words.

Word	Meaning of homophone
A. pier	to look at
B. border	one who pays to live in a house
C. sweets	another word for hotel rooms
1. core	a military term
2. swayed	a type of material
3. raise	given by the sun

ISBN: 978-1-927042-09-0

Leonardo da Vinci is one of the most famous artists of all time. Immediately coming to mind at the mention of his name are the paintings of The Last Supper, John the Baptist, and the most renowned painting in the world, The Mona Lisa. However, da Vinci was not just a great painter. He was also a visionary who drew sketches and plans for some of the great inventions of the future.

Concerned with a war raging with Venice, da Vinci designed a chariot with spear-like protrusions on each side to strike the enemy. He also sketched a drawing of an armoured car complete with wheels and a crank mechanism, arguably the first depiction of the modern-day tank.

Leonardo da Vinci –
Artist and Visionary

In da Vinci's time, Milan was filthy and overcome by a devastating plague. Da Vinci, disgusted with the conditions, designed a city with an elaborate sewage system complete with drainage. The lower level was also a place where horse stables could be housed. Da Vinci actually installed a similar design to work in Sforza Castle in Milan.

One of da Vinci's most interesting ideas was the design of a flying machine resembling a helicopter. First he designed a set of wings like those of a bird which could be attached to a person's arms. Then, he planned a machine that would feature two sets of wings attached to a long post propelled by a person sitting below pedalling. Once again, da Vinci was ahead of his time.

Da Vinci had dreamed of the possibility of humans working underwater. He designed a metal diving suit with an air bag attached. Protruding from the air bag was a tube that could be placed in the mouth, allowing the person to breathe. He also designed web-like attachments for the feet to aid propulsion underwater and a waistband filled with air to keep a person afloat.

Da Vinci may be thought of as a man born beyond his time.

ISBN: 978-1-927042-09-0

Recalling Information

A. Check the correct answers.

1. Da Vinci designed a chariot because

   A. he was interested in new forms of transportation. _____

   B. he was worried about the war with Venice. _____

   C. this was a request from the Duke of Milan. _____

2. The most famous painting by da Vinci is

   A. The Last Supper. _____

   B. John the Baptist. _____

   C. The Mona Lisa. _____

3. Da Vinci designed a sewage system for the City of Milan because

   A. the city was filthy. _____

   B. the current system was not working properly. _____

   C. there was too much drainage. _____

4. The sewer da Vinci designed could also be used for

   A. housing. _____

   B. storage. _____

   C. stables. _____

5. Fascinated with flight, da Vinci designed

   A. a type of jet plane. _____

   B. a type of helicopter. _____

   C. a type of glider. _____

6. Da Vinci designed his metal diving suit to allow a person to

   A. breathe, float, and move underwater. _____

   B. breathe, see, and hear underwater. _____

   C. breathe and stay warm underwater. _____

ISBN: 978-1-927042-09-0

Unit 9

Subordinate Clauses

- Unlike a phrase, a clause is a group of words that has a subject and a predicate but may not be a complete sentence. A **subordinate clause** depends on a main clause (sentence) to express a thought clearly.

  Example: If I have time, I will go shopping.

  "If I have time" is a subordinate clause because when used on its own, it does not make sense and lacks information. If the subordinate clause was used alone, it would be a fragment.

B.   Underline the subordinate clause in each of the following sentence.

1. Da Vinci designed a chariot because he was concerned with a war with Venice.

2. Whenever I exercise, I get cramps in my legs.

3. After I ran up the hill, I was out of breath.

4. The bell had rung before I arrived at school.

5. Before the teacher gave us any clues, we got the correct answer.

6. He went home although it was still early.

7. Whenever he scored a goal, he waved his arms.

8. He waited until the sun set.

9. She cut the pizza into 16 slices so that it could be shared.

10. You are not going to pass the test unless you start studying now.

11. Jason has been on the baseball team since he was 12.

12. Now that everyone has gone, we can take a rest.

13. He has to stay up late because the project is due tomorrow.

14. While they were halfway through the game, it started to rain.

ISBN: 978-1-927042-09-0

Developing New Words

C. Use prefixes and suffixes to build new words from the root words. Then write a synonym and an antonym for each of the root words.

Root Word	New Word	Synonym	Antonym
1. create	creation	devise	destroy
2. develop			
3. curious			
4. decide			
5. form			
6. serious			
7. shout			
8. correct			
9. wonder			
10. slow			
11. collect			
12. hope			
13. pride			
14. please			
15. truth			
16. scholar			

ISBN: 978-1-927042-09-0

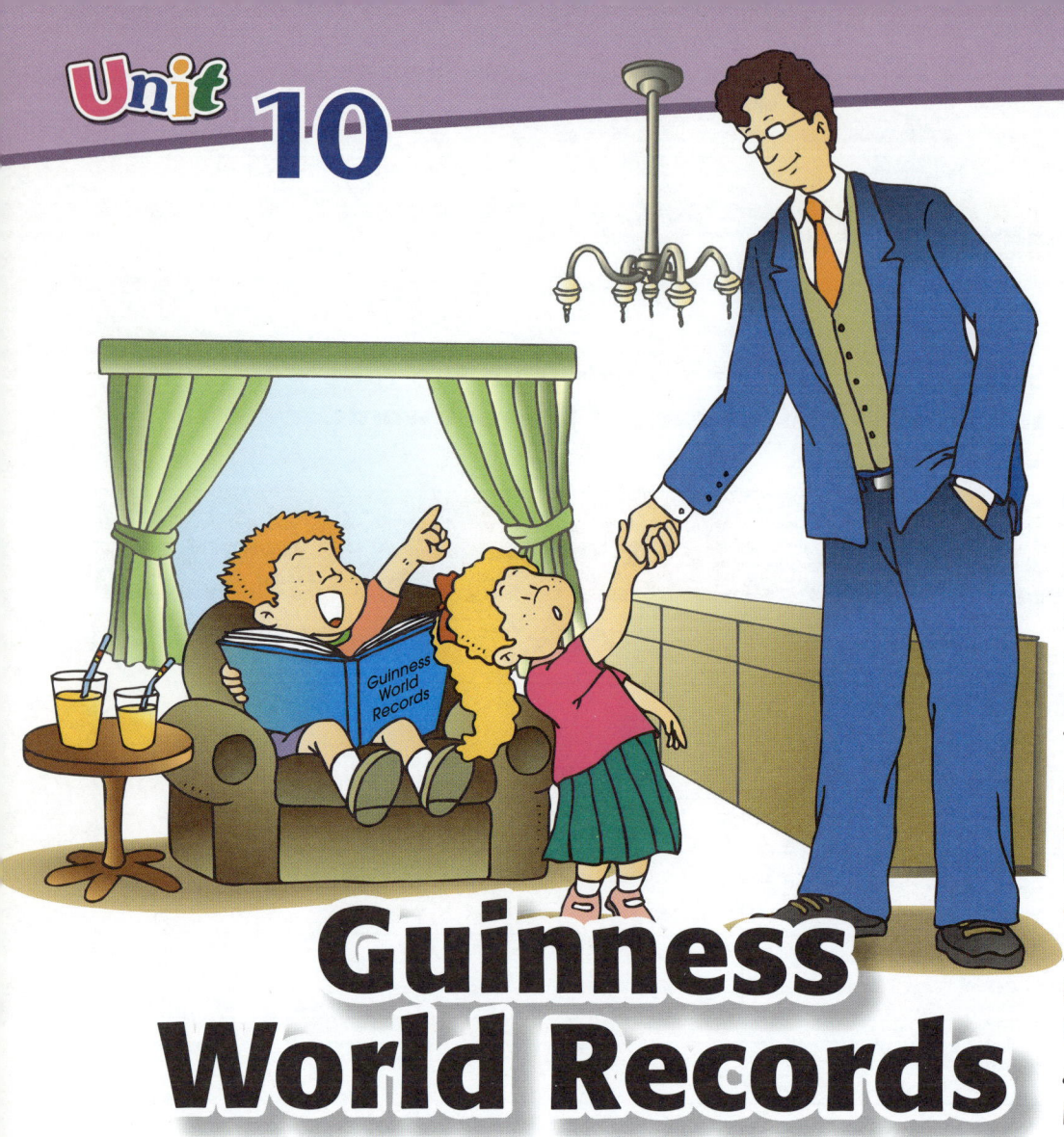

Did you know that the record for the most straws put in someone's mouth is 496 or that the tallest living person measures 8 feet 3 inches? Is it important to you to know that the oldest person ever lived to the age of 122? This information may appear useless but it was questions like these that inspired the publication of the original *Guinness Book of Records* (now known as *Guinness World Records*), named after the renowned Irish brewery.

Guinness World Records

The Guinness Brewery dates back to 1759, when Arthur Guinness established the Guinness Brewery in Dublin, Ireland. In the early 1950s, the company director at the time, Sir Hugh Beaver, found himself involved, on more than one occasion, in arguments over trivial facts. It occurred to him that pub patrons everywhere were disputing facts on a variety of topics and that a book that could offer definitive answers to such arguments would be a useful reference. Also, he realized that such a book would be a great promotional idea, so he planned to publish it and make it available to pub licensees everywhere.

Beaver approached the McWhirter brothers, who owned a fact-finding company in London, to gather facts for what became *The Guinness Book of Records*. It took over a year of painstaking research to compile and verify the information and in 1955, the first copy, a 198-page edition, was published. It became an instant bestseller and the No. 1 selling book in Britain that year. *Guinness World Records* is now published in over 20 languages, with sales exceeding 100 million copies.

The fact that *Doctor Who* is the longest-running science fiction TV series and the most home runs hit in one professional baseball season is 73 may seem trivial; however, people worldwide crave the knowledge of such seemingly insignificant facts. Many an argument can be quickly resolved by simply referring to *Guinness World Records*.

ISBN: 978-1-927042-09-0

Recalling Details

A.   Fill in the blanks with the correct words.

> 20   promotional   1955   1759   London
> Dublin   496   198   licensees   Arthur

1.   The most straws put in a human mouth is _____ .

2.   The Guinness Brewery was founded in _____ .

3.   The founder of the Guinness Brewery was _____ Guinness.

4.   The Guinness Brewery is located in _____ .

5.   The book was originally meant to be a _____ idea.

6.   Individuals who run a pub are called _____ .

7.   The McWhirter brothers' company was located in _____ .

8.   The first copy of *The Guinness Book of Records* was published in the year _____ .

9.   The first Guinness Book had _____ pages.

10. *Guinness World Records* is published in over _____ languages.

Opinions Based on Facts

B.   Answer the following questions with your opinions based on the facts in the passage.

1.   Why did the Guinness Brewery think it was a good idea, perhaps even a necessity, to devise a book of facts?

_____

_____

2.   Why do you think the book is so popular today?

_____

_____

ISBN: 978-1-927042-09-0

Noun Clauses

- A **noun clause** acts as a noun in a sentence. It may act as subject or object of a verb, or object of a preposition.

  Example 1: **Noun Clause as Subject of a Verb**

  <u>Whoever wins the race</u> will claim the prize.

  The group of words "whoever wins the race" is a noun clause acting as subject of the verb "claim".

  Example 2: **Noun Clause as Object of a Verb**

  The students did not know <u>where the meeting was</u>.

  It is "where the meeting was" that the students did not know; therefore, the noun clause, "where the meeting was" is object of the verb "know".

  Example 3: **Noun Clause as Object of a Preposition**

  The teacher was pleased by <u>how well the students were doing</u>.

  The word "by" is a preposition and "how well the students were doing" is a noun clause acting as object of the preposition.

C. **Underline the noun clause in each sentence and determine whether it functions as a subject (S), an object (O), or an object of a preposition (OP).**

1. I want to know who the tallest person in the world is. _____

2. We found where the Toyland was located. _____

3. The teacher was dissatisfied with what they did. _____

4. He asked that his name not be used. _____

5. Whatever choice is made will be fine. _____

6. Nobody told us how we could get to the destination. _____

7. We can judge our success by how we are rewarded. _____

8. What he said at the meeting was reported in the news. _____

9. Whoever bought the game could enter the lucky draw. _____

10. Don't bother me with what the program is about. _____

ISBN: 978-1-927042-09-0

New Word Forms

- Adding suffixes to root words can create new words for different parts of speech.

  Examples: "Happy + ness" becomes the noun "happiness".

  "Love + ly" becomes the adjective "lovely".

  "Sweet + ly" becomes the adverb "sweetly".

D. Circle the words in the word search that are formed from the given root words.

delicate   sense   separate   sequence   repeat   reproduce

just   require   watch   volunteer   virtue   utility   willing   peace

r	d	w	a	t	c	h	f	u	l	l	y	p
w	f	s	e	p	a	r	a	t	i	o	n	r
s	r	e	p	e	t	i	t	i	v	e	d	o
x	e	q	e	r	t	n	a	l	i	v	e	d
v	p	u	a	u	w	j	o	i	r	o	l	a
b	r	e	c	b	a	u	e	z	t	l	i	c
n	o	n	e	m	n	s	t	a	u	u	c	t
j	d	t	f	o	s	t	r	t	o	n	a	i
k	u	i	u	t	u	i	s	i	u	t	c	e
t	c	a	l	w	v	c	v	o	s	a	y	n
l	t	l	l	q	t	e	n	n	r	r	b	p
h	i	s	y	s	e	n	s	o	r	y	c	t
k	o	r	e	q	u	i	s	i	t	i	o	n
s	n	u	n	w	i	l	l	i	n	g	l	y

ISBN: 978-1-927042-09-0

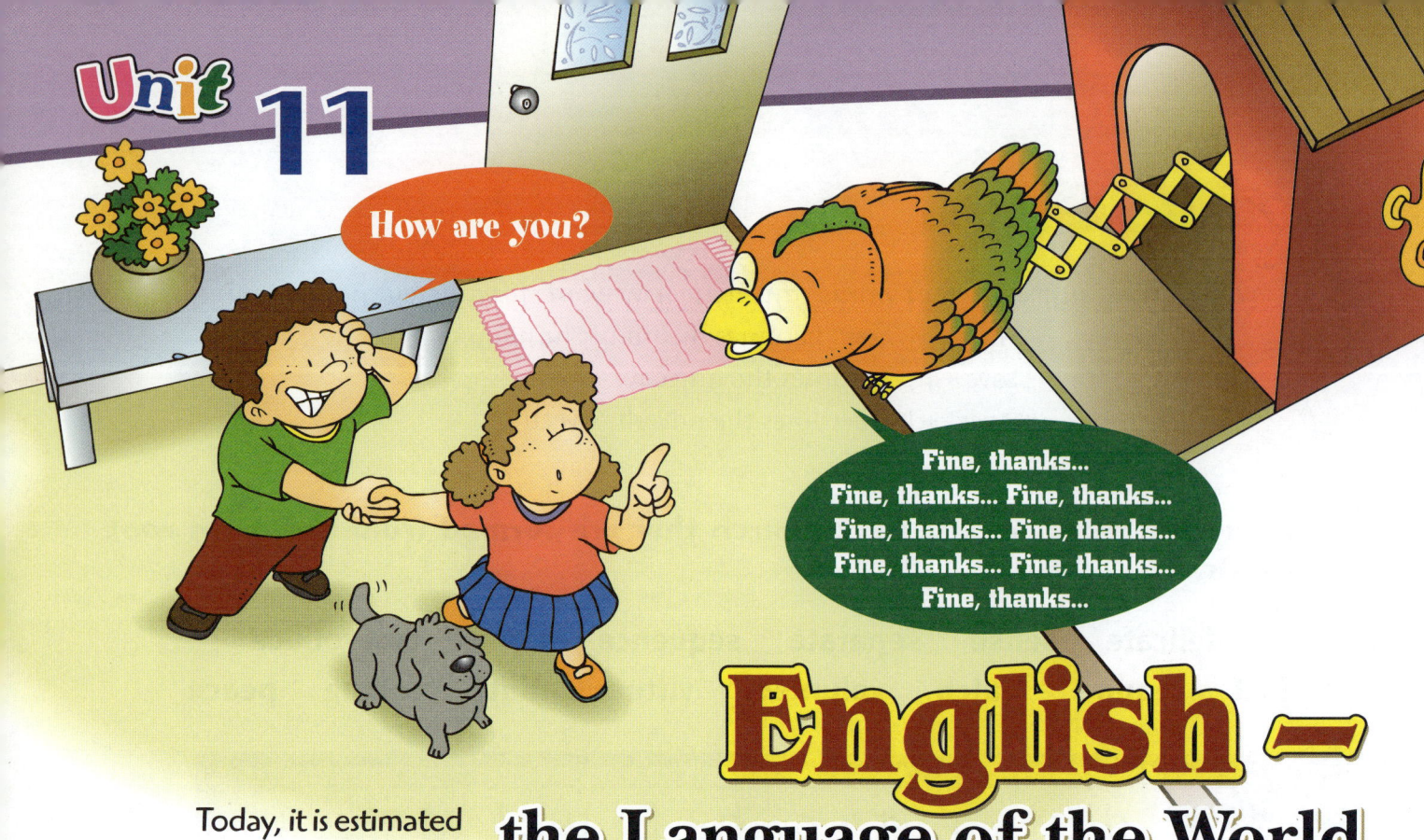

English – the Language of the World

Today, it is estimated that English is spoken by over one billion people (1/7 of the world's population) with approximately half of them having English as their mother tongue. Only Mandarin surpasses English in individual use, but no language matches English in distribution. The rise of the English language to dominance is a remarkable story. When the Roman army, led by Julius Caesar, landed in England two thousand years ago, there was no such thing as the English language. But a thousand years later, English was the native language of over six million British people. English was then spread globally to all corners of the world by military personnel, travellers, the English, Irish, Scots, and Americans who represented business and political expansion.

There is an estimate of over 6800 languages in existence in the world today, and English has by far the most extensive vocabulary. The Oxford Dictionary lists over half a million words. There is another half million of technical and scientific terms which are not included in the dictionary but are widely used. By comparison, the German language has roughly 185 000 words, while French uses approximately 100 000. English is now the language of business with over 80% of the world's telecommunications, faxes, and Internet correspondences written in English.

The most significant development of the last 100 years is the use of English as a second language by over half a billion people in countries such as India and the Netherlands. Political announcements and communications with the rest of the world promoting trade are often made in English, creating a link between non-English speaking countries and the Western world.

The desire for the world's population to learn English has spawned numerous educational agencies that arrange for English language classes in Asian countries such as China, Japan, and Korea. With the dominance of English and six billion people worldwide as potential speakers of the language, the task of providing this education is daunting.

ISBN: 978-1-927042-09-0

Fact or Opinion

A. Write "F" for fact or "O" for opinion for each statement.

1. It is estimated that over a billion people use the English language today. _____

2. More people like speaking Mandarin than English. _____

3. By the year 1000, over six million people were speaking English in England. _____

4. The English language was spread all over the world by military personnel and travellers. _____

5. There are roughly 6800 languages in the world today. _____

6. The Oxford Dictionary is the best source for learning the definitions of most English words. _____

7. English is now the language of 80% of the world's communication. _____

8. If everyone spoke English, doing global business would be easier. _____

9. Starting a school for the teaching of English is a good business idea. _____

10. Eventually, everyone in the world will speak English. _____

Using Facts to Build Opinions

B. Answer the following questions with your opinions based on the facts in the passage.

1. Why is there suddenly a surge in the need to speak English all over the world?

_____

_____

2. What is the advantage of having most of the world speak English?

_____

_____

ISBN: 978-1-927042-09-0

Compound Sentences

- A **compound sentence** is made up of two independent clauses connected by a conjunction like "and", "or", or "but".

  Example: Jackie plays many sports. Baseball is what he excels in.
  Jackie plays many sports but baseball is what he excels in.
  (The two independent clauses are joined by the conjunction "but" to form a compound sentence.)

C. Write compound sentences by joining the two sentences using "and", "or", or "but".

1. Lilian's mother tongue is French. She also speaks fluent English and Spanish.

    _____

2. Did she forget about the party? Was she sick?

    _____

3. The storm lasted all night. We stayed awake.

    _____

4. He should hurry. He will be late.

    _____

5. Sometimes you win. Sometimes you lose.

    _____

6. The players tried hard. They lost the game anyway.

    _____

7. Some students went out for lunch. Others stayed at school.

    _____

8. You cannot cure a cold. You can take medicine for relief.

    _____

9. You can buy the new game. You have to pay for it yourself.

    _____

ISBN: 978-1-927042-09-0

Building New Words

D. **Fill in the blanks with the correct forms of the words in parentheses.**

Example: There were two _____ (divide) in the hockey league.

Change the word "divide" to form the new word "divisions" which suits the meaning of the sentence.

1. English was spread (globe) _____ to every corner of the world by military personnel and travellers.

2. He will (creative) _____ a new piece of art for the display.

3. The (script) _____ on the trophy included his name.

4. She enjoyed the (action) _____ in group discussions.

5. The (gallop) _____ horse sped by the racing fans.

6. (Tight) _____ the lid to avoid spillage.

7. His desire to be famous was (wish) _____ thinking.

8. He bought the latest (verse) _____ of the computer game.

9. The (success) _____ businessman earned a high income.

10. The (adventure) _____ girl liked to climb mountains.

ISBN: 978-1-927042-09-0

No More Pencils...
No More Books

A familiar "end of year" chant for schoolchildren began with the words, "No more pencils, no more books". Could this also be a prophecy? Will the age of computer technology advance to the stage where books and pencils in schools become obsolete?

Before considering these questions, it is useful to reflect on the history of the computer. Its roots go back to 1822 when an Englishman by the name of Charles Babbage created a computation machine. Recognizing the need for storing information primarily mathematical in nature, Babbage attempted to develop a machine powered by a steam engine to store information on punch cards. Babbage's concept was sound but the technology available was inadequate to meet the task at hand.

The first electronic computer produced by the US Army in 1946 was named the ENIAC (electronic numerical integrator and calculator). It weighed 30 tons, and took up enough floor space to fill a normal-sized house. It was capable of performing about 5000 operations per second but because it produced enormous amounts of heat while in operation, it had to be shut down regularly to cool off.

Advancements in computer technology can be recorded in four principal generations. The first would be the vacuum tubes that were used in the ENIAC. With the invention of the transistor, the second generation of smaller, faster, and less expensive computers came on the scene. By the 1960s, integrated circuits took the place of transistors, creating the new wave of computers with expanded memory capabilities, operating at relatively high speeds. Finally, microprocessors marked the fourth generation of computers. These were smaller, faster, and cheaper initiating the beginning of computers.

Imagine a school of the future where, instead of opening their textbooks, students would log on to a network on their laptops and download the lessons for the day. Assignments would be forwarded by e-mail after full revision and spell check. Perhaps, in the future, students simply log on at home and attend "virtual" school.

ISBN: 978-1-927042-09-0

Cause and Effect

- A **cause** is the reason why something happens. An **effect** is what happens.
- An effect is the result of a cause and a cause results in an effect.

A. Write the cause or the effect for each statement.

1. Cause: _____
   _____

   Effect: Babbage created a computation machine.

2. Cause: _____
   _____

   Effect: Babbage was unable to develop a steam-powered computer.

3. Cause: The ENIAC produced enormous amounts of heat while in operation.
   Effect: _____
   _____

4. Cause: _____
   _____

   Effect: Computers of the second generation were smaller, faster, and less expensive.

5. Cause: Integrated circuits took the place of transistors.
   Effect: _____
   _____

6. Cause: The fourth generation of computers used microprocessors.
   Effect: _____
   _____

ISBN: 978-1-927042-09-0

Complex Sentences

- A **complex sentence** is made up of an independent clause with at least one dependent clause.

    Examples: When I walked home, it started to rain.
    (dependent clause) (independent clause)

    I wanted to take a walk while the sun was still out.
    (independent clause)   (dependent clause)

B. Rewrite each pair of sentences as a complex sentence.

Example: I ran quickly. I saw the dog. (when)

When I saw the dog, I ran quickly./I ran quickly when I saw the dog.

1. The ENIAC had to be shut down regularly. It produced enormous amounts of heat. (because)

    _____

2. The money was found. I looked everywhere. (after)

    _____

3. The girls played in the yard. It was recess. (when)

    _____

4. The tourists looked on. The farmer crossed the road with his sheep. (as)

    _____

5. The team scored a goal. The fans cheered wildly. (whenever)

    _____

6. It rained. My car was very clean. (before)

    _____

7. The test was easy. She went over all her answers again. (although)

    _____

8. The children were playing. Someone knocked on the door. (while)

    _____

ISBN: 978-1-927042-09-0

Word Confusion

We often confuse words that sound similar or words with similar spellings.

C. **Read the definitions of the word pairs and circle the correct words for the sentences.**

where / wear	a place / put on oneself		who's / whose	who is or who has / belonging to whom
berth / birth	a place for sleeping / being born		die / dye	pass away / change colour
accept / except	receive something / not including		addition / edition	adding / a specific version
beside / besides	next to / as well as		canvas / canvass	cloth for a tent / survey people
cloths / clothes	fabrics / what we wear		council / counsel	a group brought together / legal advice
altar / alter	a place of worship / change		assure / ensure	guarantee / make sure

1. **Where, Wear** was the first electronic computer produced?

2. **Who's, Whose** project scored an A+?

3. What is your date of **berth, birth** ?

4. She **dyed, died** her hair for the school play.

5. He will **accept, except** the award at the ceremony.

6. I found an old **addition, edition** of my favourite book.

7. Who is going **beside, besides** us?

8. We will **canvas, canvass** the neighbourhood for political support.

9. They shopped for warm **cloths, clothes** to wear in winter.

10. The defendant sought legal **council, counsel** before the trial.

11. There is nothing you can do to **altar, alter** the result.

12. I double-checked to **assure, ensure** that my passport had not expired.

ISBN: 978-1-927042-09-0

The Great Pyramid of ancient Egypt has been a mystery for centuries. How did the builders shape and transport over 2 300 000 stones without iron tools and transportation? How did they move these massive blocks that weighed several tons? Why did they go to so much trouble?

In attempting to answer these questions, it is important to understand how the Egyptians related to the world around them. The Egyptians observed the phenomena of nature. They believed in the balance of all things. Sunrise gave way to sunset and nature revolved in repetitive cycles. They were staunch believers in gods. The gods controlled nature and therefore controlled their lives. The Egyptians believed in life after death. Similar to the cycles of nature, they believed that they too followed a cycle: birth, life, death, and afterlife. They believed that at death their bodies were transported to a place they called the Land of the Dead, where a person could carry on with the rest of his or her existence. To facilitate this transition, they buried their dead with a variety of household tools and items of importance that would make things easier in the afterlife.

The Egyptians believed that pharaohs were direct descendants of the gods and were responsible for the order in their lives. Upon their death, pharaohs would enjoy life forever with the gods. It was believed that the pharaohs would cruise the skies watching over their people. Therefore, the pharaohs were even more important to the people after they died.

When the pharaoh Khufu ascended to the throne, he declared himself to be the manifestation of both the gods, Horus and Ra. A claim like this had never been made before. The Egyptians were overwhelmed and they declared Khufu the greatest pharaoh of all time.

The Great Pyramid of
ANCIENT
EGYPT (1)

ISBN: 978-1-927042-09-0

Sequence of Events

A. For each pair of statements, check the one that appears first in the passage.

1. ___2___ A. Pharaoh Khufu declared himself to be the manifestation of both the gods, Horus and Ra.

    ___1___ B. Upon their death, pharaohs would enjoy life forever with the gods.

2. ___1___ A. The Great Pyramid of ancient Egypt has been a mystery for centuries.

    ___2___ B. It is important to understand how the Egyptians related to the world around them.

3. ___1___ A. They were staunch believers in gods.

    ___2___ B. Therefore, the pharaohs were even more important to the people after they died.

4. ___2___ A. They declared that Khufu was the greatest pharaoh of all time.

    ___1___ B. They believed in the balance of all things.

5. ___1___ A. The Egyptians observed the phenomena of nature.

    ___2___ B. The Egyptians believed that pharaohs were direct descendants of the gods.

Your Idea

B. Answer one of the three questions in the first paragraph of the passage.

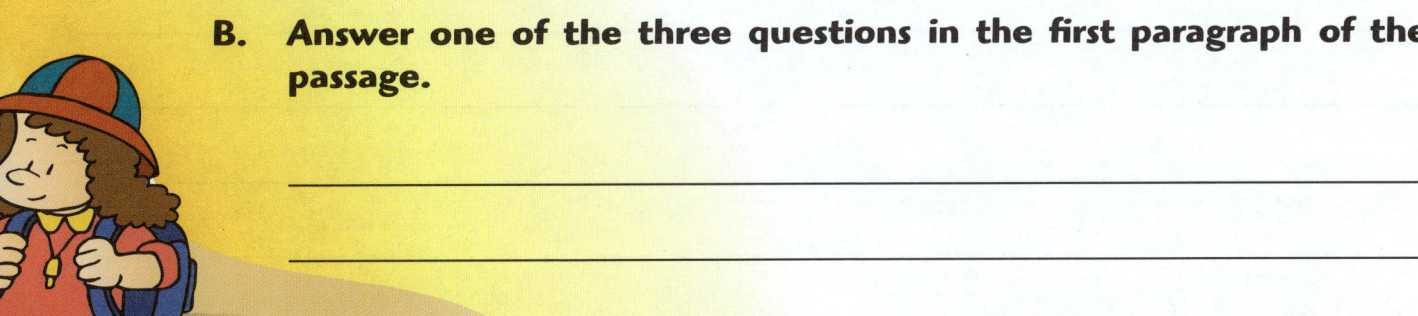

_____

_____

_____

_____

ISBN: 978-1-927042-09-0

Compound-Complex Sentences

- A **compound-complex sentence** is made up of at least two independent clauses and at least one dependent clause.

  Examples: <u>You can have my apple pie</u> or <u>you can order a sundae</u> <u>if you want something cold</u>.
        (independent clause)   (independent clause)   (dependent clause)

  <u>While I was shopping with my mom</u>, <u>I saw my friend</u> but <u>she did not see me</u>.
        (dependent clause)   (two independent clauses)

C. **Rewrite the following paragraph using varied, interesting sentence structures.**

Follow these steps:

- *Combine the sentences by creating compound, complex, or compound–complex sentences.*
- *Avoid repeating terms.*
- *Use adjectives, adverbs, and phrases to replace sentences.*
- *Change short sentences to dependent clauses.*

The Annual Play Day

This year, our school play day was held on a Friday. Parents volunteered. Teachers volunteered. Parents, teachers, and some Grade 6 students planned the games and activities. The activities were fun. The play day began at 9:00 a.m. The play day ended at 4:00 p.m. Hundreds of children attended. Hundreds of children enjoyed the day very much. There was a bake sale. The clown blew up balloons. The clown handed the balloons to the children. The older students ran the games. The parents ran the bake sale. They raised lots of money.

_____

_____

_____

_____

_____

_____

ISBN: 978-1-927042-09-0

Word Analogies

- A **word analogy** shows the relationship between a pair of words and the parallel relationship between two word pairs. By understanding the relationship of the first pair of words, you can figure out the other pair of words that follows the same pattern. Word analogies can be created using different kinds of relationships.

  Examples: Happy is to happiness as sad is to sadness. (grammatical relationship)
  Happy is to laugh as sad is to cry. (cause and effect)
  Happy is to glad as sad is to unhappy. (synonyms)
  Happy is to sad as big is to small. (antonyms)

D.   Complete the word analogies.

1. England is to king as Egypt is to _____ .

2. Careful is to cautious as construct is to _____ .

3. Frog is to jump as butterfly is to _____ .

4. Stove is to kitchen as bathtub is to _____ .

5. Pencil is to write as ruler is to _____ .

6. China is to Beijing as Canada is to _____ .

7. Child is to adult as entrance is to _____ .

8. Window is to glass as nail is to _____ .

9. Direct is to director as instruct is to _____ .

10. Human is to legs as car is to _____ .

11. Cake is to dessert as coffee is to _____ .

12. Dog is to puppy as bear is to _____ .

13. Salt is to pepper as knife is to _____ .

14. Hungry is to eat as tired is to _____ .

15. Able is to ability as reliable is to _____ .

ISBN: 978-1-927042-09-0

The Great Pyramid of ANCIENT EGYPT (2)

Khufu lived luxuriously, sparing no expense in entertaining important guests and spoiling them with lavish gifts of gold, precious jewels, and silks. Khufu knew that the wonderfully pleasurable life he was leading would not last forever and that he must prepare for the afterlife with the gods. Since he had proclaimed himself the greatest pharaoh, he was compelled to back up his claim by constructing the greatest pyramid of all time.

The location of this great pyramid was important. It had to be in the Western Desert in a location close to the Land of the Dead, yet in a spot unique to him. He chose the Giza Plateau. It was the perfect location. Limestone, the mineral used for building the blocks, was found in abundance at this site. The firmness of the land provided a perfect foundation for the structure and this location happened to rise high above the landscape, creating a monumental presence for his pyramid.

Over 35 000 labourers were drawn from nearby farms to work full time on this project. Many of them became skilled craftsmen after years of work. Various kinds of stones were brought in by boat from quarries hundreds of miles away for the ornamentation of the walls, floor, and chambers. It is believed that the construction of the Great Pyramid took many years.

Khufu died in 2566 BCE. He was mummified, a process lasting 65 days, and lowered into the sarcophagus inside the pyramid. The work of devoted priests and labourers was not yet over as they then bore the responsibility of protecting the tomb and organizing ceremonies to honour the greatest pharaoh of all time.

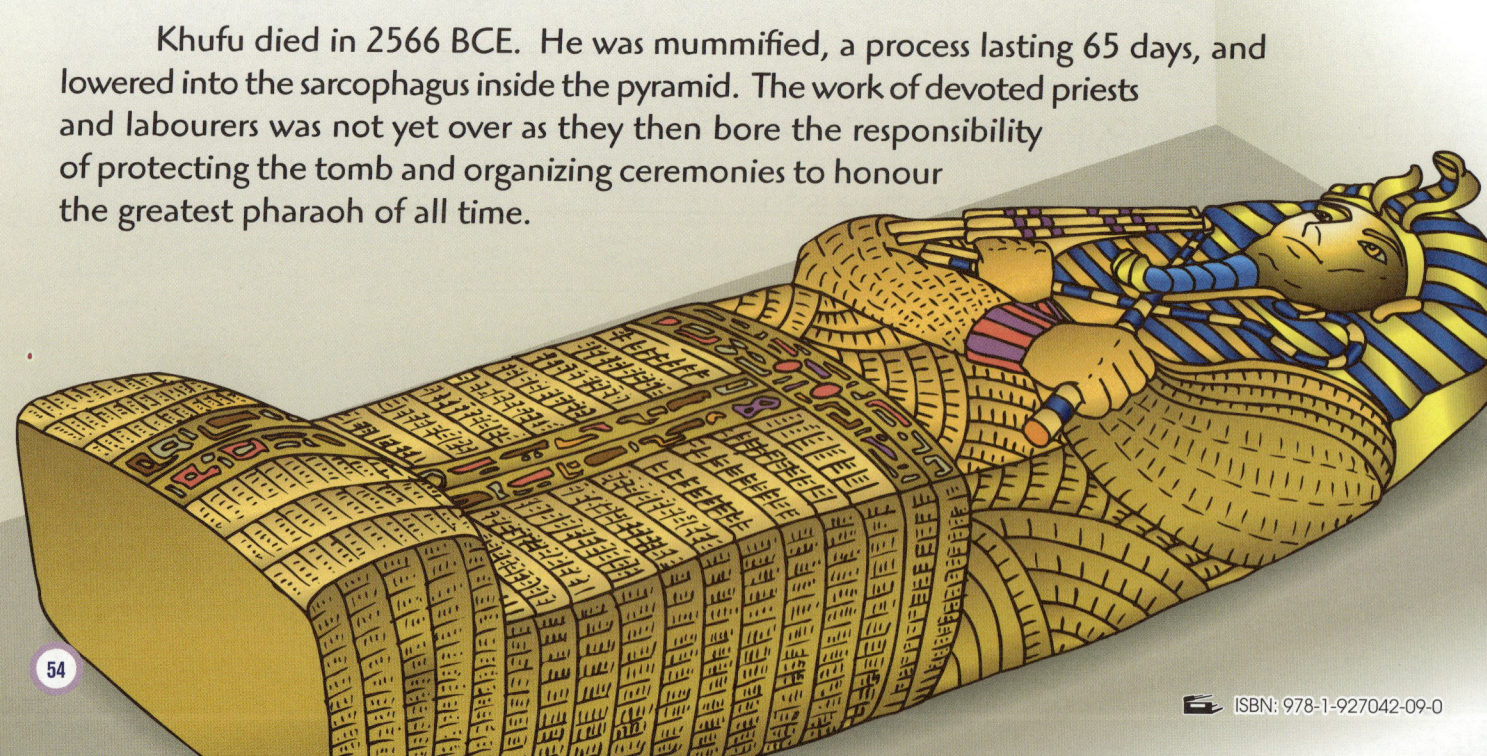

ISBN: 978-1-927042-09-0

 **Recalling Details**

A. Fill in the blanks with the correct words.

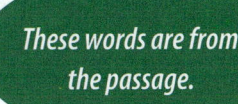 *These words are from the passage.*

afterlife   sarcophagus   farms
firmness   guests   gold   chambers
landscape   priests   construction
foundation   jewels   quarries   ornamentation
limestone   labourers   mummified

1. Khufu spared no expense when entertaining _____ .

2. Khufu prepared for the _____ because he knew that his pleasurable life would not last forever.

3. _____ was the mineral used for building the blocks used in the construction of the pyramid.

4. Khufu chose the Giza Plateau for his pyramid because the _____ of the land would support the structure.

5. The Giza Plateau rose high above the _____ .

6. Khufu needed thousands of _____ to build the pyramid.

7. The builders of the pyramid were taken from nearby _____ .

8. Boats brought in different kinds of stones for the _____ of the pyramid.

9. It took many years to finish the _____ of the Great Pyramid.

10. Khufu was _____ to preserve his body.

11. When Khufu died, he was lowered into a _____ .

12. _____ were responsile for protecting the tomb and organizing ceremonies to honour the pharaoh.

ISBN: 978-1-927042-09-0

Combining Sentences

- **Sentences** should contain a complete thought with descriptive details. A **short sentence** can be effective if it contains a singular idea that is best stated simply. Short sentences, particularly sentences with a common idea, should be combined to form longer and more interesting sentences.

- Sentences may be combined by using the following:
  a) subordinate clauses
  b) conjunctions
  c) semicolons

B. **Rewrite the following paragraph combining sentences that are common in topic.**

Use a variety of ways suggested above. Eliminate repetitious words and group the sentences that have a common topic.

In two weeks it would be Halloween. The boys and girls were preparing for Halloween. The boys and girls were making costumes. They were making costumes out of old clothes. They were having a Halloween party. The Halloween party was at the school. The Halloween party was in the gymnasium. The students in the sixth grade were doing the decorations. The students were hanging cut-outs of ghosts and witches. The students were excited. The students were looking forward to an afternoon off from regular school. There were going to be prizes. The prizes were for the best costumes. Games would be organized. There would be prizes for game winners.

_____

_____

_____

_____

_____

_____

_____

_____

ISBN: 978-1-927042-09-0

Similes

- A **simile** is a comparison of two things that have some characteristics in common. The word "like" or "as" is used to link the two things that are being compared.
- If someone is a fast runner, you might say that he runs "as fast as a deer". Or you may compare someone's singing talent to that of a bird's by saying, "She sang like a lark".
- Note the use of "like" or "as" to construct the comparison.

C. Fill in the blanks to complete the similes.

1. She was as angry as _____ .

2. He fought like _____ .

3. The plane soared like _____ .

4. The car sped by like _____ .

5. The child was as quiet as _____ .

6. The students were as happy as _____ .

Metaphors

- A **metaphor** is another form of comparison whereby two unlike things are compared to suggest a resemblance without using "like" or "as".

Examples: They swam in the sea of happiness.
The blanket of snow covered the park.

D. Underline the metaphorical terms.

1. His guidance is a light in darkness.

2. The river is the ligament to the inland.

3. Happiness is the sunshine in life.

4. The inspector's eyes were darting searchlights.

5. The main road is the artery of the town.

ISBN: 978-1-927042-09-0

With more than 1000 patented discoveries to his credit, Thomas Edison was one of the greatest scientists who profoundly shaped modern technology. However, when Edison was young, no one expected him to excel in life.

When he was seven, Edison's family moved from Ohio to Michigan in the United States after his father landed a carpentry job at a military post. Edison entered school in Port Huron but he did not do well as a student.

Thomas Edison –
the Greatest Inventor in History

Because of hearing problems, he had difficulty following the lessons and often played truant. However, Edison did not while away his time. Instead, he used the time to read books and set up a laboratory in the basement of his home. But the smell from his laboratory was often so strong that his mother had to stop him from carrying out any more experiments at home.

At the age of 12, Edison got a job as a train boy on the Grand Trunk Railway. There, he made use of an abandoned freight car as his laboratory. He even learned how to use the telegraph and later became a roving telegrapher in the Midwest, New England, and the South of the United States, and Canada. During that time, he successfully developed a device that could transmit messages automatically. By 1869, Edison's inventions in telegraphy were widely adopted, which made him decide to leave the job and become a full-time inventor. Edison's most well-known inventions included the electric light bulb, the carbon-button transmitter used in telephone speakers and microphones, and the phonograph. In explaining how he could come up with so many inventions, Edison said, "Genius is one per cent inspiration and ninety-nine per cent perspiration."

Thomas Edison died at the age of 84 on October 18, 1931. At the time of his death, he was still doing experiments in his laboratory in West Orange, New Jersey. He clearly enjoyed his work as an inventor and lived life to its fullest.

ISBN: 978-1-927042-09-0

Recalling Information

A. Write "T" for true statements and "F" for false ones.

1. Edison's father was once a scientist.   _____

2. Edison had difficulties in hearing.   _____

3. Edison worked for a railway company when he was 12.   _____

4. The electric light bulb was the only thing invented by Edison.   _____

5. Edison was doing experiments when he died in New Jersey.   _____

B. Answer the following questions.

1. Why did Edison skip classes?

_____

2. How can we tell that Edison had a passion for learning even when he skipped classes?

_____

3. Why couldn't Edison continue with his experiments at home?

_____

4. What skills did he pick up while working as a train boy?

_____

5. What prompted Edison to leave the job as a roving telegrapher?

_____

Your Opinion

C. Why is it that "Genius is one per cent inspiration and ninety-nine per cent perspiration."?

_____

_____

ISBN: 978-1-927042-09-0

D. Rewrite the following wordy sentences in a more concise way.

1. The reason Edison often played truant was that he had hearing problems.

    _____

2. He noticed the key which was in the lock.

    _____

3. The fact is that I really enjoy going to the movies.

    _____

4. In fact, I feel that exercise is beneficial.

    _____

5. In my opinion, I think that the fact is that the school year is too long.

    _____

6. On account of the fact that today is a holiday, most stores are closed.

    _____

7. According to what I remember, he won the championship last year.

    _____

8. The girl who is standing there and who is with a dog is my classmate.

    _____

ISBN: 978-1-927042-09-0

Synonyms

- **Synonyms** *are words that have similar meanings.*
  Examples: *happy – merry; large – big; small – tiny*

E. **Circle the synonym for each of the lead words.**

1. often	seldom	never	frequently	once
2. difficulty	easy	problem	importance	necessity
3. profoundly	deeply	easily	quickly	happily
4. expected	believed	respected	thought	anticipated
5. start	stop	continue	finish	begin
6. modern	present	old	moderate	out-dated
7. well-known	notorious	significant	famous	clear
8. discoveries	uncovers	covers	experiments	inventions

Antonyms

- **Antonyms** *are words that are opposite in meaning.*
  Examples: *long – short; beautiful – ugly; cold – warm*

F. **Find an antonym from the passage for each of the following words.**

1. manually _____   2. receive _____

3. detested _____   4. stationary _____

5. abandoned _____   6. fail _____

7. continue _____   8. stay _____

ISBN: 978-1-927042-09-0

While many countries in the world may share a common language, like English, they may differ in the language of measurement. Some countries, like the United States, use the imperial system of measurement introduced by the British, with inches, yards, gallons, etc. as measuring units. Others, like most European countries, adopt the metric system, in which units like centimetres, metres, kilometres, and litres are used. By multiplying or dividing by 10, 100, or 1000, conversions between various lengths and quantities are made easier.

Measurement, however, was not always so mathematically accurate. The foot, for example, was initially determined to be the length of a person's actual foot. The obvious problem with this measurement was the variety in length of human feet. Therefore, the foot of a noble or leader was used to standardize the length. The inch, which was the width of a thumb, was also somewhat regulated by using the body part of an authority figure.

The Romans, sticklers for accuracy, are credited with establishing the first standard mile. Using the measurement of five Roman feet to measure a pace (one step) and 1000 paces to walk a mile, they determined that one mile would equal 5000 feet as it came to be known. However, this measurement was not acceptable in England because it did not conform to the measurement of eight furlongs to a mile. A furlong, the common measurement used on farms, was 220 yards, and eight furlongs (a mile) totalled 5280 feet, the distance that is used today. England's King Henry I proclaimed that the yard should be the distance from his nose to the end of his thumb on his outstretched arm. Before Henry's declaration, the yard was the length of a girdle around the king's waist, which would have been different with the waistlines of different kings.

The British, who were the originators of this non-metric system still used by the Americans today, also switched partially to the metric system to simplify the mathematics of measurement. For the Americans to follow suit would be a costly venture but one that would be embraced by schoolchildren frustrated with the inconsistent measurement tables of inches, feet, yards, ounces, pounds, and tons.

Accurate Measurement
Was Not Always Accurate

5 feet

3 feet

ISBN: 978-1-927042-09-0

Matching Details

A. Do the matching.

Column A	Column B
1. centimetres	body part of an official
2. standardized measurement	width of a thumb
3. established the first mile	eight furlongs
4. use only the imperial system	5000 feet
5. British mile	220 yards
6. furlong	the Romans
7. Roman mile	the British
8. inch	replaced inches for measurement
9. began the imperial system	the Americans

Drawing Conclusions

B. Answer the following questions.

1. Why is the metric system considered an easier measurement system to use? Give an example of using the measurement.

_____

_____

2. Why would it be costly for the Americans to switch to the metric system?

_____

_____

ISBN: 978-1-927042-09-0

Overloaded Sentences

- **Sentences** become **overloaded** when we fail to create the necessary sentence breaks. Remember, a sentence contains a complete thought and although we can make our sentences more interesting by adding phrases and clauses, we must be careful not to create overly long sentences.

- The paragraph below contains overloaded sentences. Read the paragraph and the revised one. Note the changes.

2 sentences —

> The class party was scheduled for the last Friday in December before the Christmas break and all the students were excited because we were drawing names for presents and no one knew who had drawn his or her name. Finally, the day of the party arrived and the excitement was building until we were able to go and get our gift from under the tree and try to guess who had bought the gift for us.

↓

become

↓

5 sentences —

> The class party was scheduled for the last Friday in December before the Christmas break. All the students were excited because we were drawing names for presents and no one knew who had drawn his or her name. Finally, the day of the party arrived. The excitement was building until we were able to go and get our gift from under the tree. We tried to guess who had bought the gift for us.

C. Revise the following paragraph, adding in the necessary sentence breaks.

We were packed and ready to go to the airport early in the morning because our flight was scheduled for 7:00 a.m. and we were told to be there two hours ahead of time. Luckily, there was no traffic on the roads and we arrived on time to check in at the airline desk where they took our baggage and gave us our boarding passes. Soon, we were on the plane and on our way to our holiday destination that promised to be a wonderful vacation spot that would always be remembered.

_____

_____

_____

_____

_____

_____

_____

ISBN: 978-1-927042-09-0

Descriptive Language

- Your writing may be enhanced by using vivid language to replace ordinary, less colourful words.

   Example: The word "big" might be replaced by "huge", "enormous", or "gigantic", or a word such as "leave" might be replaced by "depart" or "abandon".

D. Replace the underlined words with the correct descriptive words.

abandon	cavernous	embraced	overwhelmed	staring

1. Switching from the imperial system to the metric system would be <u>welcomed</u> by many. _____

2. Katherine has been <u>looking</u> at the picture for an hour! _____

3. The <u>large</u> canyon could not be crossed. _____

4. Everyone was <u>filled</u> with excitement upon hearing the news. _____

5. The crew had no choice but to <u>leave</u> their ship. _____

E. Fill in the blanks with the correct descriptive words.

refresh	swooped	enjoy	cool	peaceful
towering	green	leaned	gentle	flowed

The 1._____ river 2._____ calmly through the 3._____ valley. On either side of the river grew 4._____ oaks whose branches swayed and 5._____ toward the riverbank.

Birds 6._____ down to dip their beaks and 7._____ a drink of 8._____ water. Forest animals also cautiously approached the bank to 9._____ themselves. Life in the valley was 10._____ .

ISBN: 978-1-927042-09-0

The names "Bermuda Triangle" or "Devil's Triangle" as it is referred to by some are unofficial titles for the triangular area of the Atlantic between Miami, Florida, Bermuda, and San Juan, Puerto Rico. The area covers over a million square kilometres of ocean and is notorious for the unexplained disappearances of numerous ships, small craft, and airplanes. The most notable is the mysterious vanishing of the entire US Navy flight squadron, Flight 19.

There are two schools of thought on these disappearances. One is the popular belief that supernatural forces were at play. Some theorize that the devil was doing his handiwork. Some theorize that aliens sucked up both the craft and the occupants through a vacuum-like funnel hurling them into space and whisking them away to another planet. One thing is certain: there were very strange forces at work during these disappearances, and logical theories and explanations have fallen short of satisfying the skeptics.

A more rational way of thinking is to consider the many natural explanations. This part of the Atlantic is subject to sudden storms. The Gulf Stream, which flows through this part of the Atlantic, can swiftly erase evidence of disasters at sea. The ocean floor in this area is a mixture of shoals and deep trenches, creating unpredictable marine conditions. In addition to environmental factors is the concept of human error. People travel in this area in craft that are too small to withstand the conditions, and without the experience to respond adequately when conditions change.

The US Coast Guard prefers to dispel any notion of supernatural or extraterrestrial forces at play. It prefers to adopt the rational viewpoint that human error, natural forces, and coincidence are factors responsible for these unsolved disasters. However, the mysterious disappearance of Flight 19 and the haunting pleas of the disoriented flight leader of that mission, Lt. Taylor, strongly suggest that there was more than nature at work on that fateful December day in 1945.

The Mystery of Flight 19 (1)

ISBN: 978-1-927042-09-0

Recalling Facts

A. Write "T" for true statements and "F" for false ones.

1.   The other name for the Bermuda Triangle is Danger Zone.   _____

2.   The Bermuda Triangle is located between Miami, Bermuda, and San Juan.   _____

3.   The Bermuda Triangle is the official name of this location.   _____

4.   One of the strangest disappearances was that of Flight 19.   _____

5.   Some people believe aliens captured the missing vessels.   _____

6.   There are no possible natural causes of the disappearances.   _____

7.   Human error is considered a possible explanation for the disappearances.   _____

8.   The US Coast Guard believes that supernatural forces were at play in the Triangle.   _____

9.   Lt. Taylor was not concerned by the strange events in the Triangle.   _____

Using Information to Form Opinions

B. Summarize the "two schools of thought" which attempt to explain the strange occurrences in the Bermuda Triangle.

1.   Natural Causes:

_____

_____

2.   Supernatural Causes:

_____

_____

3.   Which do you believe is true? Explain.

_____

_____

ISBN: 978-1-927042-09-0

 **Faulty Sentences**

- A **comma splice** is a common error in forming sentences. This occurs when two thoughts are fused together without one of them being converted into a subordinate clause.

  Example: The boy ran up the hill, he was really tired.
  In this example, the second thought is tacked onto the first and separated by a comma. There are a few ways to fix this problem:

- First, use a conjunction.
  The boy ran up the hill and he was really tired.

- Second, change one thought to a subordinate clause.
  The boy was really tired because he ran up the hill.
  After the boy ran up the hill, he was really tired.

- Third, use a semicolon. This allows you to connect two principal clauses that have a common idea giving equal importance to each.
  The boy ran up the hill; hence he was really tired.
  Notice the addition of the sentence connector.

C. Repair the following comma splices.

1. The game was over, we left the arena together.

    _____

2. They were shopping for a gift, they could not find one they liked.

    _____

3. The recess bell sounded, the schoolchildren played in the yard.

    _____

4. The dog barked at the mailman, he delivered the letters.

    _____

5. The runners took their positions, the race was on.

    _____

6. The teacher spoke loudly, we still could not hear him.

    _____

ISBN: 978-1-927042-09-0

Homographs

- **Homographs** are words that have the same spelling but different meanings. While some homographs have the same pronunciation, others are pronounced differently.

  Examples: Birds wake up at the first sign of morning <u>light</u>. (from the sun)
  Christine walked her dog in the <u>light</u> rain. (not heavy)

  The present has a lovely <u>bow</u> on it. (a type of knot)
  The civilians were reminded to <u>bow</u> as the royal procession passed through the village. (bend the upper body)

D. Circle the meaning of the underlined word in each sentence.

1. There are two <u>schools</u> of thought on the mysterious disappearances in the Bermuda Triangle.

   A. where children study   B. groups of people having the same belief

2. Sasha's <u>back</u> was hurt during the martial arts tournament last weekend.

   A. return   B. rear part of the body, from neck to hip

3. I cannot wait to enter the <u>contest</u> for I know I have a good chance of winning!

   A. competition   B. argue

4. They questioned the <u>suspect</u> for over four hours but he still did not confess to the crime.

   A. doubtful   B. person thought to be guilty

5. To <u>conduct</u> the orchestra is not an easy task.

   A. personal behaviour   B. lead

6. The movie we saw last night was a remake of another classic <u>film</u>.

   A. movie   B. thin, transparent sheet

7. My sister is <u>content</u> with her job as a music teacher.

   A. satisfied   B. subject matter

8. The differences were so <u>minute</u> that we did not notice them at first.

   A. very small   B. unit of time

ISBN: 978-1-927042-09-0

The Mystery of Flight 19 (2)

On December 5, 1945, five Avenger torpedo bombers carrying a crew of 14 left the Naval Air Station at Fort Lauderdale, Florida on a routine training flight. None of the crew members returned home and none of the five planes were found. Of the 14 members on this fateful flight, 13 were trainees. Their mission was to practise bombing at a location 60 miles east. Once the practice mission was completed, they were to continue in an easterly direction for approximately another 70 miles, turn north for 70 miles, and then turn southwest and head for home. In effect, they were unwittingly travelling a route that resembled the formation of the Bermuda Triangle.

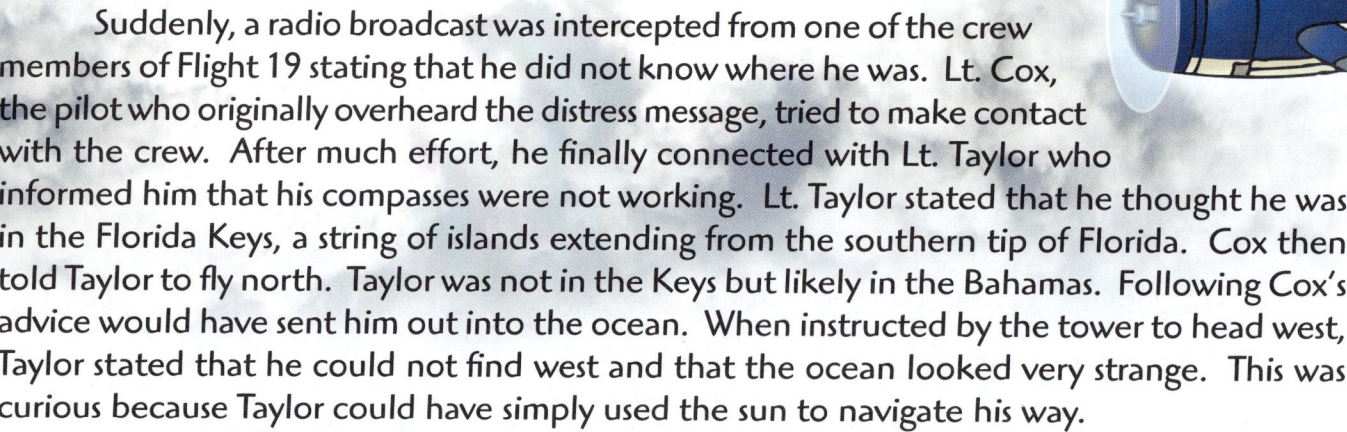

Suddenly, a radio broadcast was intercepted from one of the crew members of Flight 19 stating that he did not know where he was. Lt. Cox, the pilot who originally overheard the distress message, tried to make contact with the crew. After much effort, he finally connected with Lt. Taylor who informed him that his compasses were not working. Lt. Taylor stated that he thought he was in the Florida Keys, a string of islands extending from the southern tip of Florida. Cox then told Taylor to fly north. Taylor was not in the Keys but likely in the Bahamas. Following Cox's advice would have sent him out into the ocean. When instructed by the tower to head west, Taylor stated that he could not find west and that the ocean looked very strange. This was curious because Taylor could have simply used the sun to navigate his way.

The Navy sent out the Martin Mariner flying boat with a crew of 13 to search for Flight 19. It too disappeared. Now there were 27 people missing. With the sun setting and radio transmission failing, the Fort Lauderdale Naval Base became increasingly concerned for the safety of the members. Fuel in the aircraft was running low and to complicate matters further, a storm was moving into the area. At 7:00 p.m., Taylor made his final radio transmission. Search and rescue crews fought through stormy weather for most of the night in a desperate attempt to find any evidence of the fate of Flight 19 and the Martin Mariner. No trace of either was ever found.

ISBN: 978-1-927042-09-0

 **Listing Facts**

A. **List three important facts for each paragraph in the passage.**

1. *Paragraph One*

_____

_____

_____

2. *Paragraph Two*

_____

_____

_____

3. *Paragraph Three*

_____

_____

_____

Using Facts to Build an Argument

B. **Suppose your task is to prove that supernatural forces were the real causes of the disappearances in the Bermuda Triangle. List the most important facts that you would use to build your case.**

1. _____

2. _____

3. _____

4. _____

5. _____

6. _____

ISBN: 978-1-927042-09-0

 **The Narrative Paragraph**

- A **narrative paragraph** gives information, tells a story, or explains something to the readers. It should have a beginning, a middle, and a conclusion.
- The beginning should have a topic sentence that stimulates the readers. It should set up the story by giving introductory facts or information so that the readers can understand the writer's purpose.
- The middle sentences should give all the details.
- The concluding sentence should summarize the purpose of the narrative.

C.   Write a narrative paragraph using one of the following topic sentences.

a.   Riding a bicycle is not only good exercise, it is also a great means of transportation.

b.   In the neighbourhood, there are many ways to earn money by doing odd jobs.

c.   My summer holidays are always full of wonderful experiences.

d.   Christmas season is my favourite time of the year.

ISBN: 978-1-927042-09-0

Frequently Misspelled Words

- *Some words are frequently misspelled. These words are not unusual or particularly difficult. Some of these words sound or look proper even when spelled incorrectly.*

D. Circle the correctly spelled word in each pair.

1.	massacre	massacer	2.	monitor	moniter
3.	separate	seperate	4.	fourty	forty
5.	heros	heroes	6.	barely	bearly
7.	goverment	government	8.	existense	existence
9.	seize	sieze	10.	atheletic	athletic
11.	emporer	emperor	12.	wether	whether
13.	ninth	nineth	14.	calendar	calender
15.	independant	independent	16.	kangaroo	kangeroo
17.	rythm	rhythm	18.	truely	truly
19.	embarrassed	emberassed	20.	luckly	luckily
21.	occasion	ocassion	22.	develope	develop
23.	receive	recieve	24.	accommodate	accomodate
25.	tution	tuition	26.	imaginary	imaginery

ISBN: 978-1-927042-09-0

ISBN: 978-1-927042-09-0

1   The Monarch Butterfly

A. 1. T   2. F
    3. T   4. F
    5. F   6. F
    7. T   8. T

B.   (Suggested answers)
    1. The Monarch starts as a caterpillar. Then it becomes a pupa with a hard capsule. Finally, it emerges as a fully-grown adult butterfly.
    2. The great mystery about the Monarch butterfly is that it travels up to 3000 km one way to reach its winter roosts.

C. 1. Monarch butterflies do not fly (at) night.
    2. He sat (in) the kitchen and ate the entire cake (by) himself.
    3. He kicked the soccer ball (through) the goalposts.
    4. The members (of) the team played hockey (against) another team.
    5. He enjoyed the movie (with) the scary ending.
    6. Get the ball before it goes (on) the road.
    7. (Of) all (of) her friends, she liked Susan best.
    8. The pianist played the piano (for) all the people.
    9. John and Anne were late (for) school.
    10. Never before had he worried so much (about) his school grades.
    11. Please put this box (into) the drawer.
    12. He is thinking (of) an interesting title (for) his new book.

D.
    1. fire   work
    2. mail   way
    3. out   place
    4. when   storm
    5. wild   less
    6. wind   grow
    7. home   box
    8. rain   ever
    9. drive   mill
    10. care   life

E.   (Suggested answers)
    fire: firewood, campfire, firefly, fireworks, wildfire
    home: homesick, homeland, hometown, homegrown, homecoming

2   Foxes - the New City Dwellers

A. 1. wolves and dogs
    2. by night
    3. the red fox
    4. ten kilometres
    5. rabbits, mice, and rodents
    6. 50 km per hour
    7. 10 to 12 years
    8. in the middle of winter
    9. wild fruit and grass
    10. retraces its steps and hides in trees

B.   (Individual writing)

C. 1. be seen
    2. was stung
    3. has been decorated
    4. will come
    5. were collected
    6. have
    7. has left
    8. is helping
    9. was given
    10. was cancelled
    11. will be closed
    12. dined

D. 1. uncommon
    2. inadequate
    3. disrespect
    4. undependable
    5. independent
    6. disappear
    7. immature
    8. displeased
    9. uncertain
    10. immortal
    11. unreliable
    12. distasteful
    13. inappropriate
    14. irresponsible
    15. disregard
    16. disbelief

3   "The Great One" - Wayne Gretzky (1)

A. 1. six   2. his father
    3. ten   4. one
    5. Gordie Howe   6. 17
    7. 215

B.   (Individual answers)

C. 1. had established
    2. has not eaten
    3. has already put
    4. had finished
    5. have not asked

ISBN: 978-1-927042-09-0

6. had already started
7. has not visited
8. has never been
9. have joined

D. 1. debut
2. shatter
3. compensate
4. instilled
5. oversized
6. prodigy
7. opportunity
8. insurmountable
9. avid
10. consecutive
11. incorporated
12. surpassing
13. imitating
14. astounding
15. milestone

4   "The Great One" – Wayne Gretzky (2)

A.   (Suggested answers)
Paragraph One: Gretzky led the Los Angeles Kings to the Stanley Cup finals and boosted the attendance at home games.
Paragraph Two: In a Celtics-Lakers basketball game, Gretzky met Janet Jones, who later became his wife.
Paragraph Three: Gretzky expressed admiration for past and present hockey greats and listed five players for his personal All-Star Team.
Paragraph Four: Gretzky had the uncanny ability to control the offence of the game, which made him such a great player.

B.   (Individual answers)

C. 1. IN
2. SUB
3. IN
4. IM
5. IM
6. IN
7. SUB
8. SUB
9. IM
10. IN

D.

(crossword puzzle)
- A. KNACK
- B. FOREIGN
- C. WITNESS
- D. AMBASSADOR
- E. UNCANNY
- 1. EXHIBITED
- 2. STATURE
- 3. AUTOBIOGRAPHY
- 4. EMBRACED
- 5. DISAPPOINT

5   The Sasquatch – Canada's Legendary Monster

A. 1. F   2. F   3. T   4. F
5. F   6. T   7. F   8. T
9. T

B. 1. It is called "Bigfoot" because of the large bare footprints it leaves in the mud.
2. The Sasquatch could only survive by hiding in the day and coming out at night.
3. (Individual answer)

C. 1. Mrs. Green said that Roger Patterson had seen a Sasquatch in 1967.
2. Nina told her dad that there was a stranger outside.
3. Mom always says that money is not everything.
4. Kyle explained that there are no polar bears in the South Pole.
5. Sarah told her friends that she had won the competition.
6. My sister told me that Vienna is the capital of Austria.

D. 1. wickedly
2. simply
3. purely
4. confinement
5. glorious
6. treacherous
7. definitely
8. discovery
9. invention
10. heavily
11. happiness
12. performance
13. creative
14. majority
15. reality
16. anchorage

6   Left Brain, Right Brain

A.   (Individual answers)

B. 1. hemispheres
2. lateralization
3. 12%
4. 10%
5. touch
6. right

C. 1. Writing with the left hand ; S
2. Missing the game ; S
3. taking the cable car to the peak ; C
4. Swimming in the ocean ; S
5. eating too much fried food ; O
6. raking fallen leaves in the yard ; O
7. composing a memory book ; C
8. solving the problem on your own first ; O
9. reading science fiction ; C
10. doing volunteer work ; C
11. working out at least four times a week ; C
12. Getting into an abandoned house in the middle of the night ; S

ISBN: 978-1-927042-09-0

D. 1. unique   2. visual
    3. determine   4. experiment
    5. population   6. stationary
    7. perception   8. hemispheres
    9. lateralization

7   The Jackie Robinson Story (1)

A. 1. F   2. F   3. F   4. O
    5. F   6. O   7. O   8. F
    9. O   10. O   11. F   12. O
B.   (Individual answer)
C. 1. ✔   2.   3. ✔   4. ✔
    5. ✔
D.   (Individual writing)
E. 1. appear   2. unknown
    3. poor   4. dull
    5. unsociable   6. flexible
F. 1. antibody   2. antisocial
    3. antiseptic   4. antifreeze
    5. antiaircraft

8   The Jackie Robinson Story (2)

A. 1. In California, Robinson attended Pasadena Junior College where he set records in track and field, quarterbacked the football team, and led the basketball team in scoring.
    2. When he joined the Kansas City Monarchs of the Negro League, he was finally being paid to do what he did best.
    3. Branch Rickey, a forward-thinking Dodger manager, signed Jackie Robinson to a contract and sent him to play for the Montreal Royals, a Dodger farm team.
    4. Robinson answered the public scorn by winning the Rookie of the Year in 1947 and going on to help the Dodgers win six pennants in ten years.
B.   (Individual answers)
C. 1. to sign a major league baseball contract ; Adj
    2. to let in fresh air ; Adv
    3. to search for their dog ; Adv
    4. to improve her skill ; Adv
    5. to gather information for their project ; Adj
    6. to raise funds for the organization ; N
    7. To give up ; N
    8. to stay fit ; Adj
    9. to meet the king and queen in person ; Adj
    10. To keep experimenting ; N
    11. to complete the activity ; Adv

    12. to get all the ingredients ready ; N
D. 1. great   2. watt
    3. read   4. sale
    5. brake   6. feat
    7. pours   8. bear
E.

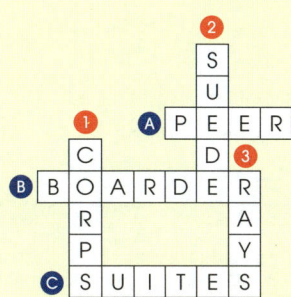

9   Leonardo da Vinci – Artist and Visionary

A. 1. B   2. C   3. A   4. C
    5. B   6. A
B. 1. because he was concerned with a war with Venice
    2. Whenever I exercise
    3. After I ran up the hill
    4. before I arrived at school
    5. Before the teacher gave us any clues
    6. although it was still early
    7. Whenever he scored a goal
    8. until the sun set
    9. so that it could be shared
    10. unless you start studying now
    11. since he was 12
    12. Now that everyone has gone
    13. because the project is due tomorrow
    14. While they were halfway through the game
C.   (Individual answers)

10   Guinness World Records

A. 1. 496   2. 1759
    3. Arthur   4. Dublin
    5. promotional   6. licensees
    7. London   8. 1955
    9. 198   10. 20
B.   (Suggested answers)
    1. Pub patrons liked disputing facts on various topics and it would help if there was a book with definitive answers to such arguments.
    2. People worldwide crave the knowledge of seemingly insignificant facts.

ISBN: 978-1-927042-09-0

C.
1. who the tallest person in the world is ; O
2. where the Toyland was located ; O
3. what they did ; OP
4. that his name not be used ; O
5. Whatever choice is made ; S
6. how we could get to the destination ; O
7. how we are rewarded ; OP
8. What he said at the meeting ; S
9. Whoever bought the game ; S
10. what the program is about ; OP

D.

r	d	w	a	t	c	h	f	u	l	l	y	p
w	f	s	e	p	a	r	a	t	i	o	n	r
s	r	e	p	e	t	i	t	i	v	e	d	o
x	e	q	e	r	t	n	a	l	i	v	e	d
v	p	u	a	u	w	j	o	i	r	o	l	a
b	r	e	c	b	a	u	e	z	t	l	i	c
n	o	n	e	m	n	s	t	a	u	u	c	t
j	d	t	f	o	s	t	r	t	o	n	a	i
k	u	i	u	t	u	i	s	i	u	t	c	e
t	c	a	l	w	v	c	v	o	s	a	y	n
l	t	l	l	q	t	e	n	n	r	r	b	p
h	i	s	y	s	e	n	s	o	r	y	c	t
k	o	r	e	q	u	i	s	i	t	i	o	n
s	n	u	n	w	i	l	l	i	n	g	l	y

11 English – the Language of the World

A.
1. F   2. O   3. F   4. F
5. F   6. O   7. F   8. O
9. O   10. O

B.   (Individual answers)

C.
1. Lilian's mother tongue is French but she also speaks fluent English and Spanish.
2. Did she forget about the party or was she sick?
3. The storm lasted all night and we stayed awake.
4. He should hurry or he will be late.
5. Sometimes you win and sometimes you lose.
6. The players tried hard but they lost the game anyway.
7. Some students went out for lunch and others stayed at school.
8. You cannot cure a cold but you can take medicine for relief.
9. You can buy the new game but you have to pay for it yourself.

D.
1. globally   2. create
3. inscription   4. reaction
5. galloping   6. Tighten
7. wishful   8. version
9. successful   10. adventurous

12 No More Pencils...No More Books

A.
1. Babbage recognized the need to store mathematical information.
2. Technology was not available.
3. It had to be shut down regularly.
4. The transistor was invented.
5. New computers with expanded memory capabilities operating at relatively high speeds were created.
6. Smaller, faster, and cheaper computers became available.

B.
1. The ENIAC had to be shut down regularly because it produced enormous amounts of heat.
2. The money was found after I looked everywhere./After I looked everywhere, the money was found.
3. The girls played in the yard when it was recess./When it was recess, the girls played in the yard.
4. The tourists looked on as the farmer crossed the road with his sheep./As the farmer crossed the road with his sheep, the tourists looked on.
5. The fans cheered wildly whenever the team scored a goal./Whenever the team scored a goal, the fans cheered wildly.
6. My car was very clean before it rained./Before it rained, my car was very clean.
7. Although the test was easy, she went over all her answers again./She went over all her answers again although the test was easy.
8. While the children were playing, someone knocked on the door./Someone knocked on the door while the children were playing.

C.
1. Where   2. Whose
3. birth   4. dyed
5. accept   6. edition
7. besides   8. canvass
9. clothes   10. counsel
11. alter   12. ensure

ISBN: 978-1-927042-09-0

13 The Great Pyramid of Ancient Egypt (1)

A. 1. B   2. A   3. A   4. B
   5. A
B.   (Individual answer)
C.   (Individual writing)
D.   (Suggested answers)
   1. pharaoh   2. build
   3. fly   4. bathroom
   5. measure   6. Ottawa
   7. exit   8. metal
   9. instructor   10. wheels
   11. drink   12. cub
   13. fork   14. rest
   15. reliability

14 The Great Pyramid of Ancient Egypt (2)

A. 1. guests   2. afterlife
   3. Limestone   4. firmness
   5. landscape   6. labourers
   7. farms   8. ornamentation
   9. construction   10. mummified
   11. sarcophagus   12. Priests
B.   (Individual writing)
C.   (Individual answers)
D. 1. is a light in darkness   2. is the ligament
   3. is the sunshine   4. were darting searchlights
   5. is the artery

15 Thomas Edison – the Greatest Inventor in History

A. 1. F   2. T   3. T   4. F
   5. T
B. 1. He had difficulty following the lessons.
   2. He used the time to read books and did experiments at home.
   3. The smell from his laboratory was too strong.
   4. He learned how to use the telegraph.
   5. He decided to be a full-time inventor.
C.   (Individual answer)
D.   (Suggested answers)
   1. Edison often played truant because of hearing problems.
   2. He noticed the key in the lock.
   3. I really enjoy going to the movies.
   4. Exercise is beneficial.
   5. I think that the school year is too long.

6. Today is a holiday so most stores are closed.
7. I remember he won the championship last year.
8. The girl who is standing there with a dog is my classmate.

E. 1. frequently   2. problem
   3. deeply   4. anticipated
   5. begin   6. present
   7. famous   8. inventions
F. 1. automatically   2. transmit
   3. enjoyed   4. roving
   5. adopted   6. excel
   7. stop   8. leave

16 Accurate Measurement Was Not Always Accurate

A.

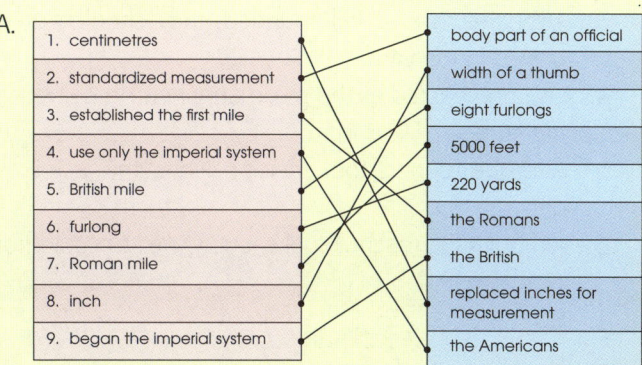

B. 1. Conversions between various lengths and quantities are made easier by multiplying or dividing by 10, 100, or 1000.
   2. (Suggested answer)
      The switch would affect all aspects of life.
C.   (Individual writing)
D. 1. embraced   2. staring
   3. cavernous   4. overwhelmed
   5. abandon
E. 1. gentle   2. flowed
   3. green   4. towering
   5. leaned   6. swooped
   7. enjoy   8. cool
   9. refresh   10. peaceful

ISBN: 978-1-927042-09-0

17   The Mystery of Flight 19 (1)

A. 1. F   2. T   3. F   4. T
    5. T   6. F   7. T   8. F
    9. F

B. 1. This part of the Atlantic is subject to sudden storms and the Gulf Stream can erase evidence of disasters swiftly. Also, the ocean floor there creates unpredictable marine conditions.
    2. It was either the devil doing his handiwork or aliens that hurled the craft and the occupants into space.
    3. (Individual answer)

C.   (Suggested answers)
    1. When the game was over, we left the arena together.
    2. They were shopping for a gift but they could not find one they liked.
    3. After the recess bell sounded, the schoolchildren played in the yard.
    4. The dog barked at the mailman when he delivered the letters.
    5. After the runners took their positions, the race was on.
    6. Although the teacher spoke loudly, we still could not hear him.

D. 1. B   2. B   3. A   4. B
    5. B   6. A   7. A   8. A

18   The Mystery of Flight 19 (2)

A.   (Suggested answers)
    1. Five Avenger torpedo bombers left the Naval Air Station. Their mission was to practise bombing. None of the crew members returned.
    2. One of the crew members of Flight 19 stated on radio that he did not know where he was. Lt. Taylor thought he was in the Florida Keys. Taylor was not in the Keys but likely in the Bahamas.
    3. The navy plane in search of Flight 19 also disappeared. Fort Lauderdale Naval Base became increasingly concerned for the safety of the crews. No trace of Flight 19 or the search plane was ever found.

B.   (Individual answers)

C.   (Individual writing)

D. 1. massacre   2. monitor
    3. separate   4. forty
    5. heroes   6. barely
    7. government   8. existence
    9. seize   10. athletic

11. emperor   12. whether
13. ninth   14. calendar
15. independent   16. kangaroo
17. rhythm   18. truly
19. embarrassed   20. luckily
21. occasion   22. develop
23. receive   24. accommodate
25. tuition   26. imaginary

ISBN: 978-1-927042-09-0